Praise for *Pieces of My Mother*

"Melissa Cistaro has written a vivid and unforgettable first memoir. She writes with true compassion, exposing the delicate, complicated bond between mothers and daughters."

—*New York Times* bestselling author Ayelet Waldman

"This is an astonishing book, full of heartbreak and love and hard-won wisdom. Melissa Cistaro writes beautifully not just about her search for the mother who abandoned her, but about the myriad ways parents and children don't and do connect. Told in vivid scenes and through the texts of letters her mother never sent, Cistaro chronicles a journey that goes way past forgiveness to true understanding."

—Will Schwalbe, bestselling author of *The End of Your Life Book Club*

"Sometimes we are defined as much by the person who is missing as the person who is there. Melissa Cistaro has a story to tell and one you don't hear every day. I was deeply moved from word one."

—Kelly Corrigan, bestselling memoirist of *The Middle Place*, *Lift*, and *Glitter and Glue*

"*Pieces of My Mother* is driven by an almost tangible need for clarity. To understand and accept herself, the writer must first unravel the mystery of her mother. Amidst the chaos of life and loss, in clear lovely prose, Melissa Cistaro has written the perfect memoir. I love this book."

—Abigail Thomas, bestselling author of *A Three Dog Life*, *Safekeeping*, and *What Comes Next and How to Like It*

"Melissa Cistaro's imagery is startling and vivid, her story brutally honest and devoid of judgment. Pieces of My Mother is a story that lingers in the heart long after the last page is turned."

—Hope Edelman, bestselling author of Motherless Daughters and The Possibility of Everything

"An honest and affecting story of the many complexities involved with family relationships."

—Kirkus Reviews

"Full of hope, regret, and lessons learned, Pieces of My Mother is a unique and compelling look at how profoundly mothers affect our lives. Whether absent or hauntingly close, longing for a mother can force a child into maturity beyond her years, and garner her with a lifetime of longing. This book is as lyrical as it is honest, as humorous as it is heartbreaking."

—Monica Holloway, bestselling author of Cowboy & Wills and Driving with Dead People

"Filled with moments of poignancy and grace, Melissa Cistaro's beautiful book lands on a gorgeous note of redemption. I loved it."

—Lolly Winston, bestselling author of Good Grief and Happiness Sold Separately

"I read this book in one uninterrupted, lump-in-the-throat sitting. Equal parts memoir and emotional whodunit, Pieces of My Mother is a beautiful, wrenching story, meticulously crafted. Cistaro understands all too well the fallibility of memory, the desire to be a flawless mother, and the fear of having inherited the gene for the opposite."

—Katie Hafner, author of Mother Daughter Me

"In an age where the pressure to be the perfect parent is beyond fierce, enter Melissa Cistaro with a clear-eyed look at a real family. Pieces of My Mother is about how it is to be a mother and a daughter in the imperfect world we all actually live in. A heartbreaking and heart affirming first book."

—Peter Orner, author of Last Car Over the Sagamore
Bridge, Love and Shame and Love, and Esther Stories

"Weeks after I read the last gorgeous page of Pieces of My Mother, I still find myself thinking about Melissa Cistaro and her complex, maddening, and fascinating mother. What caused this woman to walk out of her house one afternoon, leaving the children she loved behind? As Melissa puts the pieces together we are treated to an outstanding memoir written with tenderness, wit, and depth."

—Elaine Petrocelli, Book Passage

"Pieces of My Mother is part memoir, part detective story, and throughout its pages riveting to read…A brave and impressive debut."
—Tom Barbash, critically acclaimed author of Stay Up With
Me and the New York Times bestseller On Top of the World

"Readers will feel Melissa Cistaro's anxiety over her own role as a parent, in light of her lifelong sorrow over her mother's abandonment of the family. Detailed memories, honest reflection, and true insights into her mother's life combine in this spell-binding memoir of what it means to be a loving mother and a good daughter."

—Cheryl McKeon, Manager, Book Passage

"Melissa Cistaro's luminous memoir is full of heart, wisdom, and suspense...a page turner, impossible to put down. It's also filled with the kind of writing that makes you catch your breath in awe."

—Barbara Abercrombie, author of
A Year of Writing Dangerously

"Truly wonderful. Not your typical dysfunctional family memoir. I thought the structure—alternating scenes of her dying mother with the past was brilliant."

—Suzy Staubach, University of Connecticut
Co-operative Bookstore

"Challenged to piece together a woman she barely knows, Cistaro takes the reader into her world, her story. Weaving between Now and Then, Cistaro tells of life with and without her mother."

—April Gosling, Boulder Book Store

pieces of my mother

a memoir

melissa cistaro

Published by Sourcebooks, Inc.
P.O. Box 4410, Naperville, Illinois 60567-4410
(630) 961-3900
Fax: (630) 961-2168
www.sourcebooks.com

Library of Congress Cataloging-in-Publication Data
Cistaro, Melissa.
  Pieces of my mother : a memoir / Melissa Cistaro.
    pages cm
(hard cover : alkaline paper) 1. Cistaro, Melissa. 2. Cistaro, Melissa—Childhood and youth. 3. Cistaro, Melissa—Family. 4. Mothers and daughters—United States. 5. Abandoned children—United States—Biography. 6. Absentee mothers—United States—Biography. 7. Mothers—United States—Death. 8. Mothers—United States—Correspondence. 9. Olympia (Wash.)—Biography. I. Title.
  CT275.C597A3 2015
  306.874'3—dc23
                                    2014040808

Printed and bound in the United States of America.

WOZ10987654321

For my family—past and present

author's note

This story is a work of nonfiction and is drawn from memory, letters, early recollections of my childhood, and family lore. Some names and time sequences have been changed. The letters of my mother are written verbatim and at times condensed. Undoubtedly, there are things I've remembered differently than others, but this is the only version I know. This is my attempt to put the pieces back together.

THEN

a house underwater

Bun-Bun notices my mom outside before I do. He tells me about it. We watch her walk toward her car. She's wearing her summer dress that is the color of ripe avocados. Her brown purse, slung over her shoulder, is as fat as the raccoon that crawls into our garbage cans late at night, and she has an armful of clothes hooked into her elbow. Her favorite coat drops onto the pavement. It doesn't look like a coat the way it crumples up on the ground.

I know that coat so well, every bit of tan, brown, yellow, and red—every small wooden button. So many times I have traced the curling patterns and small rows of dots with my fingertip, and my mom always reminds me that the pattern is called "paisley." She turns around, picks up her favorite paisley coat, and tosses it on top of the pile of clothes she's already put in the backseat of her blue car, then slams the car door shut.

As she turns around to look back at the house, I have Bun-Bun do a little wave and a dance as I duck below the window in my room. *She'll think Bun-Bun has really come to life.* His tan head and floppy ears are made of real rabbit fur that only recently began to shed around his green eyes and on the tips of his ears. I know how to make him look like he's hopping through a field. I lift my eyes just above the ledge. My mom is standing next to the car looking down at her feet.

I am supposed to be taking a nap, but it's too hot and I don't like to sleep. During nap time my whole room comes to life and anything can happen. Stuffed animals talk to each other, fairies fly out of the wall sockets, and plastic horses gallop across the hardwood floor. My brother told me that when I'm five like him, I won't have to stay in my room during nap time.

For days now the air has been like fire, so hot that it ripples above the concrete and makes things outside look like they are underwater. It is the kind of heat that has made our next-door neighbor's dogs hide underneath our house where it's cool and dusty. Mr. Bird, who owns the dogs, came over and told us this just yesterday.

"Dogs know what to do with themselves when California heats up like this, but not people," he said. "It's the kind of heat that could cause some folks to snap." And when he said that word, "snap," he took the toothpick out of his teeth and broke it in two. Then he laughed like he thought he was clever. Later, I saw his broken toothpick on our porch and kicked it into the dead grass where it got lost in all the yellow.

I open my bedroom door and peer into the living room. My brother Eden is asleep on the couch with a box of Lucky Charms wedged underneath his arm. The TV is on and I watch for a moment as Underdog flies across the gray screen, and I remember that my brother Jamie isn't here. He's almost six and the oldest. He left the house earlier to go swimming in his friend Bobby

Winston's pool. My mom was mad when Mrs. Winston showed up early to grab Jamie for swimming. She told Mrs. Winston that she only had two cigarettes left and didn't want to go out to the store in the heat.

When Mom is out of cigarettes, she counts on Jamie to be here with Eden and me so she can run down to the corner market. If she has to wait too long to get them, the house begins to swell with noise—the clap of cupboards opening and closing, the crack of the ice-cube tray slamming against the counter, and her voice rising over ours like a mockingbird.

I wish that Mrs. Winston had offered to lend her some cigarettes or get her some, but she didn't. She just pointed to her hairdo, which she called a "beehive," and said, "This darn heat is just killing me and my hair too."

After Mrs. Winston left, my mom said she thought that hairstyle looked "goddamn ridiculous." I picked up the box of cigarettes lying on the table and carried it to my mom. She tapped the last two out of the package. Then we sat side by side on the plaid couch as she smoked each of them. Out of her red shiny lips came rings of smoke like little white doughnuts floating through the air. I reached up and stuck my finger through the center of one. She pulled my arm away and whispered, "No, just watch."

She said she liked it when the rings began to lose their shape and stretch out. She said they were beautiful the way they disappeared. I didn't like it when they went away. I preferred it when they first came out of her red lips and looked like powdered doughnuts.

"Make more," I said. And she did, like magic, over and over.

With my brother Eden asleep and Underdog ducking back into

a telephone booth, I sneak past them and into the kitchen where our old fan is clunking around in circles, but no cool air is coming out. On the counter there is a pitcher of sticky orange Kool-Aid with three black flies floating on the surface. The sight of the soggy flies makes me uneasy, and in an instant, the heat feels like it will swallow me. I want my dad to come home from work.

I race back to the window in my room to see if my mom is coming back in. She is standing in the same place. I want to tell her that it is too hot out there for her, that she could melt. But she's stuck out there, it seems, and I'm stuck in here.

I need her to come back in the house. I need her to tell me that nap time is over and that tonight we will go to Fosters Freeze where the ice cream races out of a noisy machine and into perfect swirls of vanilla and chocolate.

Instead, she opens the car door and gets in. I lay my hand against my bedroom window. The glass is warm and it feels like I can almost reach her.

I know this is not a trip to get cigarettes.

I want to yell out to her: "Please don't leave…" I am trying to say it. But nothing comes out. I just watch her without blinking once. Bun-Bun and I both have stupid plastic eyes and sewed-on mouths. Inside of us there is nothing but sawdust.

Then I see her mouth break open wide like a fish gasping for air. She is crying inside her car. The air wobbles above the concrete. Everything is underwater. It crosses my mind that I could swim to her if I knew how. Jamie does; he would swim to her if he were here.

I press my forehead against the glass and swallow every word I know. Underwater, everything is quiet and full of ripples. My mom is a mermaid as she swims away from me, her thick hair waving like strands of long seaweed. I don't hear the sound of the car engine starting up, but I watch as my mom backs up and drives away in her baby-blue Dodge Dart.

———

Jamie says he was bad and that's why Mom left. Eden cries the most and spends extra time in the backyard looking for gypsy moths and black crickets to kill. I collect small boxes from around the house—empty Band-Aid tins, Lipton Tea containers, and Lucky Strike matchboxes. They are tiny suit-cases that I can hide things in. Anything I want: buttons, bad thoughts, daisy petals, and even the shiny sequins that fall off my Christmas stocking. I put these small boxes just beneath my windowsill, all lined up and in order, and keep them there so that I can show them to my mom when she comes back.

Our dad tells us she's taking "a break" from us for a while but he doesn't like to talk about it. Jamie says maybe we will see her when the weather cools down. Or maybe she will come if one of us has a birthday. I keep hoping it is all a mistake. When I hear laughing late at night outside our house, I stay awake in case it is her coming back. And sometimes I hear the radio next door shouting out songs she would sing along to. I can feel her sway-ing me in her arms and singing "Good-bye, Ruby Tuesday." I am waiting for her to come bolting through the front door and never stop hugging us again.

A sitter, who is not our mom, comes to live at our house so our dad can go back to work. And when that sitter gets tired of us, a new one arrives. Everyone says I am too young to remember what's happened and that children my age simply don't remember the details. I can't blame them for saying that. But I am as quiet as a cat, watching everyone and everything.

NOW

a house in los angeles

2003

My sandals clap across the hardwood floor and into the blue room where my children sleep. There are school art projects that dangle from clothespins, Legos in every color, stuffed animals of every breed, and shelves full of books. A small night-light flickers in the corner of the room. My seven-year-old son is already asleep on the top bunk. My little girl has called me back in for the third time. I remind myself to be both patient and firm. She is four.

"Yes, Bella?"

"Mama, I keep thinking about the scary cat with red eyes."

"Have you tried thinking of all things blue?" I ask, hoping she'll be soothed by our nighttime ritual of naming all the things in the world that could possibly be blue.

"Yes. I tried that. I can't sleep," she says with a whimper. She reaches out and pulls at my arm. I do not feel the patience in me tonight.

"Mama, can you stay with me on my bed? Please?"

She doesn't understand that I am goddamn tired. My husband is out of town, as he is so often these days. I know that if I lie down, I won't be able to get back up. My mind is on the school lunches

I haven't yet made, the stacks of dishes lined up all the way around the kitchen counter, and the wet towels that are beginning to smell because they haven't made it into the dryer yet. And then there are the twenty-four shamrock place mats that I promised to cut out for the preschool class tomorrow and the haircut appointment I need to cancel.

I look out to the yellow light in the hallway. The headache that began this afternoon in my neck is now settling in behind my eyes. I rub my left eyebrow back and forth, trying to chase the pain away. I can't do this drawn-out routine with Bella. I can't do the twenty questions, not tonight. *Okay,* I think, *take a deep breath and count to ten.* That's what all the parenting books say to do. I need to come up with something—some kind of sleeping dust from the sandman, some magic spell from Wynken, Blynken, and Nod.

"How about if you close your eyes and think of great names for pets? And not just the name of the pet, but you also have to think of what the pet looks like—in detail."

She stares up at me, her eyebrows furrowed. "But that might make me think of the cat."

Her mind never settles. If she were like her big brother, the routine would be a bedtime story, a back scratch, and off to slumberland. But not Bella. She is a girl with an epic imagination.

"Bella, please. It's time to sleep."

"I'm trying," she protests.

I watch her eyes blink, and tuck the covers snug around her body. I place her velvet bear underneath her chin and her shaggy cat in the crook of her arm. As I lean down to kiss her goodnight, her eyes pop open wide and stare at me.

"Mama, what did your mom do when you were scared?"

Her question catches me off guard.

The room seems to tilt sideways. I don't feel dizzy, but heavy—like I might not be able to stand on my own two feet. I recognize it, this feeling, this physical sensation of being pulled backward, like standing in the undertow at Stinson Beach.

I do not recall slipping off my sandals and lying down alongside Bella on her bed. But suddenly I am here next to her, staring up at the ceiling with its tiny glow-in-the-dark stars. *Star light. Star bright. First star, I see tonight. Wish I may, wish I might, have this wish I wish tonight.*

"Mama," she asks again, "what did your mom do when you were scared?"

"I can't remember, Bella." My body is stiff on the bed. I am trying so hard to do the right things, to be a good mother. "I didn't get scared much," I say. That's not the truth either. "I guess she tucked me in and said things to help me to feel safe. Sort of like the things I say to you."

My mouth aches. I am a coward. I am afraid of the undertow. I don't want her to know that sometimes a mother can't stay. "Let's close our eyes and go to sleep," I whisper to her.

She smiles, pleased that I am lying on her bed, then whispers a reminder, "Don't leave, Mama." The room tilts again; the ceiling stars go blurry. *The words I never once said.*

I cannot tell Bella that my mom left when I was a little girl. And yet it was a simple fact, a well-memorized statement when I was growing up. "My mom doesn't live with us," I'd say in the same way I'd say, "Lilacs are my favorite flowers." It didn't occur to me that becoming a mother myself could wash to shore the wreckage of the past. To tell my daughter this truth is to tell myself the darkest truth. That I was leavable. Unkeepable.

I come from a long line of mothers who left their children. What if there exists some sort of genetic family flaw, some kind of "leaving gene" that unexpectedly grabs hold of mothers like the ones in my family? What if that leaving gene is lying dormant inside me? And what if my daughter, with her fretful imagination, worries that I might leave one day?

I picture my mom, a thousand miles away. She has always been a thousand or more miles away, except for the occasional visits. Each of us carried her leaving in different ways. When she left, it seemed she took all the colors with her. The world turned gray and itchy like a tight wool sweater pulled across my chest. In the early years, she didn't call us or show up on our birthdays, which deeply upset my father. He hoped she would at least acknowledge us on those special occasions. Later, she began to drift in and out of our lives like our live-in sitters, always seeming just out of our reach. If we were lucky, we might see her once—occasionally twice—a year. And then we never knew when, or if, we would see her again. Perhaps she might have stayed to hold our small hands if she could have foreseen the directions our lives would go after that summer.

How would my daughter thrive if I leaned down to kiss her good-night right now and told her that I couldn't live with her and her brother anymore? And that I wasn't sure when I'd visit next or if I'd come back? How will I ever be able to answer my daughter's questions—or my own?

I close my eyes, rearrange my unbearable thoughts, and tuck them away. *I am a mother now. A good mother.*

I rest my lips against Bella's shoulder and breathe her in like sweet, warm bread. I want my daughter to feel safe. Every day I rebuild a scaffold inside myself in hopes that she will have something sturdy to hang on to.

It's all I can do for now.

NOW

christmas day

Four Years Later

The telephone rings midmorning. Barefoot, I step outside before answering. It's my mom's sister.

"Melissa, your mom's stopped eating and she's not very—well, cognizant."

"Stopped eating," I repeat. "Okay."

No, this is not okay. I've been tracking my mom's struggle with cirrhosis and liver cancer over the past few years. I've witnessed her health deteriorating during our occasional visits, which I reached out for more frequently since she's been sick. All my fears surface. She is leaving again.

"The hospice nurse doesn't expect her to make it to the new year," says my aunt.

I bite down on my thumbnail until it snaps between my teeth and squint up at the December sun. The calculation is a simple one. New Year's Eve is in six days. Her sixty-fifth birthday is in five. Los Angeles to Seattle. I can get there before the sun sets.

I look through the window at my daughter, Bella, waving a wand in big circles inside the house. Bubbles scramble up in the air and then drift down toward her bare feet. She is almost nine now but still believes in Santa Claus and the magic of Christmas.

"Should I come?" I ask my aunt.

"I don't know. It might be too hard," she says.

I feel an odd pang of jealousy, like she wants to be the only one with my mom when she dies. But I can't explain why I need to be there either. I just know I need to see her one last time. I cannot bear the thought of her sneaking away before I arrive.

"I'm coming," I tell my aunt, acutely aware of how disappointed the kids are going to be that I'm leaving them on Christmas and also feeling that there isn't a moment to waste.

Bella pleads with me not to leave her on Christmas, "of all the days!"

"It's not fair, Mama. Can't you go tomorrow instead?"

I shake my head, unable to articulate my sense of urgency. My son, Dominic, thumbing through a deck of new playing cards, asks, "When are you coming back?"

I look out the window as if the answer is somewhere in the row of yellow and pink roses still blooming in the December sun, or in the way the palm tree casts its slender shadow against the house. I add and subtract the hours, minutes, and seconds. I have to get there before she dies.

"I don't know when I'll be back for sure." I hate that I can't give a definite time. I swore I'd never do this to my own children.

"You have to be back for New Year's Eve," cries Bella. "You have to *promise* this. Please, Mama?"

"Okay, I promise," I say as I gather a random assortment of clothes and toss them into a suitcase.

My seatmate on the flight to Seattle guzzles a ginger ale and organizes the peanuts on his tray in two neat lines. He looks to be in his early twenties, at most. I'm not usually one to engage in a conversation on a plane, but the ride is bumpy from turbulence and I can't seem to quiet my mind. I need to talk to someone, anyone.

"You live in Seattle?" I ask.

"Just outside Tacoma. I'm stationed at Fort Lewis right now," he says. "My wife is having a baby any day now."

I smile. "Ah, you must be so excited."

"Yeah." He fills his mouth with the ice cubes from his plastic cup. "And nervous. Big responsibility."

"I know. I've got two kids."

"That's cool. You going to have any more?" he asks.

I laugh at the thought. "No, my kids are big now—nine and twelve."

"I can't even imagine what that's like," he says.

Talking to this stranger about to embark on the journey of raising a child briefly lifts my spirits. The potential of birth overriding death this Christmas night is a welcome thought. I can't help but wonder if his child will be born before my mom dies—or after. Our conversation circles around until he finally asks me where I'm headed for the holidays.

"I'm going to see my mom in Olympia. She's sick. Liver cancer."

"That's rough. I'm sorry."

I turn to the window, searching for signs of light in the distance. There's nothing else to say. This opportunity to connect with my mom—at last, before she leaves—feels possible. This is what I know for sure: I want to be there when she dies. I want to hold her body. It's pathetic, this fantasy of a good-bye. But I keep imagining myself holding her hand when her body finally surrenders. Only then will I be able to touch her face and allow myself to finally feel a handful of her hair—hair that I have not dared to touch since I was a little girl. I will not contain my grief any longer. It will echo through the house. Though the woods. Past the stars. I will hold her until the sky changes its color.

Every time she left when I was a child, I had to believe in the promise of her return. I tried not to miss her, but I did. This time, my mom won't be returning, and I am terrified of my own unraveling. What kind of courage will I need when I arrive in Olympia?

As a girl, the story of Pandora—and the beautiful and dangerous box that Zeus warned her never to open—mesmerized me. I came to believe such a vessel could exist inside me, and if I dared to tip the lid, it would expose all my dark and ugly places. Throughout the years, it was safer to keep all the things I was fearful of locked inside. Now, on my way to say good-bye to my mom, I am afraid of what I've contained for so long.

The overhead seat-belt sign dings and lights up. We are closer now. The plane wobbles through the winter sky and I close my eyes, longing for those days when my brothers and I were a tribe of three.

THEN

fire and sugar

Wanna learn how to light matches, Melissa?" asks my oldest brother, Jamie, busting into my room.

"No."

"Come on. It's really cool," says Eden.

"I don't think we're supposed to," I tell him.

No one is home right now. We are four, five, and six.

"Jamie and me are gonna do it anyway," says Eden. "Besides, you better do it or we'll stuff Rice Krispies in your ear again when you're sleeping."

My skin itches when Eden says this. I don't want to wake up to the sound of snap, crackle, pop in my ear again.

"Well, okay," I say.

"You're a good sister," says Eden.

I follow my big brothers in their boxer shorts and white T-shirts downstairs to where it is cool. We huddle on the green shag carpet, the three of us like crows hanging out on a grassy field. Jamie reaches up and pulls out a pack of matches that he's hidden behind the owl painting on the fireplace. It's a creepy owl with tangerine eyes that stares at us no matter where we are in the room.

"Lemme go first," says Eden.

"No, I go first, you go second, Melissa goes third," says Jamie.

My brother pulls fire out of a matchstick so swiftly. He's an expert at it from the times he studied our mom lighting her cigarettes. I stare at the little wisp of fire like it's a lucky firefly that's guiding me. A tiny blue heart pulses in its middle.

"Now, you got to hold on to it 'til it burns to the bottom. That's the rule, Melissa."

Then Jamie hollers and flings his match across the room.

"Dang it!" he yells. The match lands on the shag carpet and he jumps on it fast. "Don't worry. It usually goes out when you throw it."

We all stare at the black spot on the green rug but don't say anything. I notice the owl staring at it too.

Jamie glares at me. "Don't tell anyone about this or you'll get in big trouble. You got it?" We nod.

The smell of smoke makes me sneeze two times in a row. I hope my dad gets home from work before it's my turn. I don't like this game.

Eden grabs the pack and tries three times before his match lights. Then he smiles big. I can see the yellow light flickering in both his eyes. He loves the fire more than any of us. He lights one after another until Jamie grabs the pack from him and hands it to me.

"You gotta tear off a match first. Then flip the cover over backward and place the match tip between the scratchy stripe and the cover, then squeeze—and pull hard," he instructs me.

I squeeze my paper match between the closed cover and pull, but drop it when the heat pushes through the paper and stings my fingertips.

"Try a new one," says Jamie.

Again, I try but the burn between my fingers is quick and sharp like a cut. I can't do it fast enough. I just get the burn, no fire, no flame. I concentrate, pull hard, throw my match, step on it—nothing.

"You're wasting all the matches, Lissa!" Eden yells and grabs the box from me.

I crawl on top of the dark blue couch and start counting the little toffee-colored dots on the fabric. Jamie and Eden argue over who gets to light the last match. They throw off their shoes and start wrestling on the carpet. My fingers sting, but I don't say a word. Maybe I should tell my dad that our new babysitter goes to see her boyfriend down the street and asks Jamie to be in charge. But Jamie says this is why she is such a good sitter.

"She trusts me," he says. "Besides, when Mom comes back to live with us, we won't need any more stupid babysitters."

Jamie says this a lot, but I've stopped believing him. I listen to the rooster clock ticking in the next room. My feet have fallen asleep underneath me and are tingly, so I wiggle them back and forth.

Then Jamie jumps up from the floor. "Hey, I know something even better than fire. You wanna get some cake, guys? I know where we can get some. Any flavor you want too."

"You better not be lying," says Eden.

"Where's the cake, Jamie?" I ask.

"Follow me, but you have to *swear* you won't tell anyone about it, okay?"

"Okay," Eden and I say at once.

"Jinx," says Eden. And I'm glad we agree on cake.

Barefoot and silent, we follow our big brother outside. We crouch down on our knees to crawl underneath the house where the dirt smells like rain and there's hardly room to stand up. Jamie says he found this secret spot and the stash when he was playing hide-and-seek. He hunches over a big brown box pushed into the corner and rips open the cardboard flaps. He pulls out smaller boxes with photographs of fluffy, frosted cakes. First I see the all-white cake with matching white frosting. Then there's a pink cake with layers of frosting the color of cotton candy. And there's even chocolate frosting on chocolate cakes and tall yellow cakes with creamy brown frosting.

"Dad gets all the free cake mix he wants 'cause he works for Duncan Hines and they are a cake-making factory," explains Jamie. "And you don't even have to cook them. They taste good right out of the box. Since you didn't get to light a match, you get first pick, Melissa."

There is no question in my mind. "I want the white one with the white frosting."

"Yep. That one's coconut." He beams and hands me the box.

Eden picks the strawberry-pink one. And Jamie smiles like he's our dad at Christmas passing out the presents.

I tear open the noisy wax bag, and white dust flies into my face. I look inside. "Where's the frosting?"

"I guess it doesn't come with the frosting. It's good without it anyway." Jamie shrugs.

I scoop my index finger deep into the bag and pull up a miniature mountain. It's cool on my finger and about to fall off. I shove it into my mouth. It's dry, white, and sugar sweet.

We shove handfuls of the sweet powder into our mouths and

laugh when it makes us cough. We tear open boxes and sample them all. We say, "Oh, try this one next" and "Oh, *this* one is the best."

My bare legs are coated with fine, white powder, and I draw a smiley face on top of my thigh. For a moment, I stop wishing my mom were still here. I'm glad there is no one to tell us not to light matches and not to sneak the boxes of cake mix. I like being here with my brothers. We're a tribe of three making a pact in the cool dirt underneath the house. There are so many colors and flavors, and after a while the cake doesn't even taste so good, but none of that matters. We've got sweet things. Fire and sugar.

NOW

arriving in olympia

S now falls, dusting the roadways and tall evergreens surrounding Seattle. It's close to midnight by the time I pull into the gravel driveway at my mom's house in Olympia. It's a two-story farmhouse set off a rural road outside town. A pack of dogs all bark in unison and greet me with bodies and tails wagging.

My aunt Joanna—an eccentric, lovely, and smart shrink who is intensely fascinated with botany and probably one of the most well-traveled people I know—appears in the front doorway. The creases around her mouth deepen into a smile of empathy. We hug. Of all the people who could be here, I'm most grateful for her presence. And I feel for her.

When my mom dies, my aunt will have lost all of her immediate family. Their brother, David, was killed in an avalanche along with six other boys when he was fifteen in one of the most tragic climbing accidents of the century. Their mother (my grandmother Joan) drank herself to death within five years of the accident. My grandfather died some years later from lung cancer. Now, Joanna will watch her only sister die from the same alcohol-related complications as their mother.

"Why don't you pop in the bedroom and see your mom?" my aunt suggests.

"How is she?"

"She's been asleep all day, but she smiled when I belted out a song we used to sing as kids."

I don't feel prepared to see my mom. I'm still trying to keep my emotions intact, and I'm uncertain where to gather fortitude right now. Maybe leaving my family on Christmas wasn't the right thing to do. Then I remind myself why I'm here and how quickly she could go.

The hardwood floor squeaks beneath my feet as I enter the room where my mom is sleeping. She is a heap of blankets. A mop of sandy hair frames her face and open mouth. Her skin is yellow gray. The folds around her eyes are as delicate as crepe paper.

Where is my beautiful mother?

My mind retreats to another day when she was a Katherine Hepburn look-alike with her intense blue eyes, swept-up hair, and taut cheekbones. I recall her confident gaze in the mirror as she painted a line of frosty blue shadow across her lids—the strap of her red camisole dangling from her shoulder. Her arms were strong then from riding horses, tending gardens, or pushing dairy cows aside on the farm where she worked one summer.

I sit next to her on the edge of the bed, keeping my voice low. "Hi, Mom. It's me, Melissa. Merry Christmas."

She opens one eye at me, the other sealed shut. Her eye, a pale blue marble, lingers on me a bit longer, and then she makes a shallow, primitive sound from her throat. Uncertain of how to help, I call out for my aunt.

She rushes in and lifts a cup of water with a thick straw to my mother's dry lips. Her mouth can barely work around the straw, and most of the water travels into the crease of her neck.

"Melissa is here to see you. She's right here, you know," my aunt attempts to explain.

No response.

"Hi, Mom, it's me." I wait. "It's me," I say again, and now I feel like a needy puppy jumping up and down, trying to get her attention. She doesn't recognize me.

"She's pretty heavily medicated," my aunt says gently. "Maybe she'll come around in the morning."

My mom doesn't recognize my face or my voice. I tell myself it's okay, even though it's not. What matters is that I've made it to Olympia. She's still alive and just as mysterious as ever.

I drag my suitcase upstairs to the office bedroom in my mom's house. There is a small bed, an old oak desk, a few hundred books, and an assortment of shells, torn butterfly wings, and small animal skulls. I sit at her work space, swivel around in the chair, and feel a rush of hopelessness in being surrounded by these bits and pieces of a life collected—a life I never really knew—and all the books she's loved.

Years ago, in an attempt to understand her, I began to put all my thoughts down in lined notebooks. Back home, I have forty-seven spiral notebooks stuffed underneath my desk. Every page circles back to my mom leaving—then and now. It's not healthy, I know. It's affecting who I am as a mother. Half of me wanders in the past, and the other half overcompensates by striving to be the perfect mother—the one who will never leave.

When I first began to fill the notebooks, I was only attempting to understand my mom's leaving. But memory is as random as the wildflowers that grew behind our yellow house—a purple lupine here, a patch of California poppies there, a circle of yellow buttercups—and hidden among them, the slivers of broken glass that sliced our feet open. I was searching for the memories that could rescue me. I believed that if I could dig up the goodness in the things that haunted me, there was a chance that I could save my mom, my brothers, my dad, myself. Now I think that if I can just get the words right on the page, maybe I can keep her alive.

When I've looked at those notebooks, it has crossed my mind more than once that I may have some kind of mental imbalance. I've read that a particular temporal-lobe tumor can bring on hypergraphia, which causes an intense and obsessive need to write. I watch for obsessive behaviors in myself because addiction bleeds from almost every branch of our family tree.

As I look around my mother's office room, I wonder about the things she has collected and chosen to keep over the years. Beneath her desk is a sturdy metal filing cabinet. I slide the file drawer open. It has the mechanics and heaviness of what I imagine a morgue drawer to be like. The scent of paper and dust flies out of the drawer, as it would from an old book that has been closed for a very long time. I feel guilty about looking in her personal files but can't resist my compulsive need for information. Anything that will help me understand the mother of mine who is downstairs dying.

My fingers move carefully through the files, respectfully, as I have learned from handling old and rare books in my job. I am mindful of their fragile bindings, the brittle paper, and the sometimes uneven deckle edges.

My mom's distinct handwriting—a spirited mixture of cursive and print—is scrawled across the tabs of every folder. Something about her handwriting makes me cry. As I move my hand across the file folders, the skin on my head suddenly feels taut. I raise my hand and feel along my scalp for the raised bumps of skin where the stitches went in so long ago. The day she finally came back to visit when I was five years old.

THEN

one at a time

My mom hits the brakes too hard, too fast. My head flies forward into the black dashboard, but I am too stunned to cry out.

"Goddamn it!" she yells.

"What? What happened, Mom?" Jamie calls from the backseat.

"Jesus fucking Christmas, lady!" screams my mom out the window, waving a cigarette in her right hand. The ashes land in a soft clump on my knee.

"Did you hit her car, Mom?" Eden pipes up.

"No, but Jesus, I should have! She stopped for no good reason that I can see."

I reach up under my hair where I feel something stinging. Eden pops up behind me from the backseat and sees the blood when I pull my fingers away.

"Ahhhh…Melissa is bleeding!" he yells.

My mom turns to me, her bright blue eyes opening wide. "Oh my God, are you all right, honey? Where's the blood coming from?" Her dangly earrings sway back and forth and shimmer like silver fish. I feel dizzy.

"Where are all those goddamn napkins we got from Doggie

Diner?" she yells to my brothers as she yanks the car over to the curb on Nineteenth Avenue and turns it off.

Jamie pulls out a handful of white napkins that he and Eden have stuffed into the crack between the seats. I don't want the Doggie Diner napkins to get wrecked. We got them special to save, and now the red dog head on the napkin is going to be ruined.

I look in the small, round mirror outside my window. My blond hair is smeared with bright blood the color of cherry cider. Dad is not going to be happy about this. This is the first visit that we have had with my mom since I turned five. This is a very, very important day.

When Dad told me just yesterday that Mom was coming to take us to the San Francisco Zoo, I knew right away we had to be good. This was the day she could change her mind and come back to live with us. Maybe that's what she was going to tell us at the zoo—that she couldn't stand being away anymore and that she missed us too much.

But things didn't go very well at the zoo. When we got there, the gorillas started throwing their poop through the fence at us. After that, Jamie and Eden behaved very badly and fought like monkeys. Jamie got caught shooting a rubber band at the rhinos. He said he did it because rhinos have tough skin and wouldn't feel it. Then Eden had a fit when the seagulls stole his pink popcorn square and my mom didn't have money to get him a new one. I wanted him to stop his crying because it was making Mom smoke a lot of cigarettes. We left early because she said the way we were acting embarrassed her. Eden threw his arms around her legs and screamed for her to let us stay longer. She yelled and called him a crybaby.

I keep the napkins pressed to my head as we drive to the hospital. Eden and Jamie are so quiet in the backseat that it scares me. I look back at them, the wind blowing their hair in all directions, and I wish I knew what they were thinking. I wish we could go back to Doggie Diner, before the zoo, get more red dog napkins, eat more hot dogs with fancy mustard, and start the day all over—but I have a feeling our mom isn't going to take us to Doggie Diner ever again.

When we arrive at the hospital, a nurse with crooked lipstick looks in my eyes and talks very slowly to me like I am a pet dog about to run away. She tells me that I will need stitches, but only a few.

"Mom, please, I don't want stitches," I plead. She puts her hand on mine and promises me it will be okay.

When the doctor arrives, my mom proudly tells him that I haven't cried once since this happened.

"That's a good slice. She's very brave," the doctor says.

My mom smiles at him and then at me. I don't like the words "good slice."

"Do you know the song about Rudolph the red-nosed reindeer, Melissa?" the nurse asks me in her slow voice. I nod.

"Okay, you're going to sing that song while the doctor puts the stitches in, and it's going to be over very quick," she says.

I don't feel like singing; it's not even Christmastime. The nurse presses her hand, slippery with lotion, against my cheek to keep my head from moving.

"Sing," she says.

"Rudolph the red-nose…"

That's as far as I get. I feel the needle going into my skin and then the tugging of the thread. It's not okay to be sewed into, and I hate the nurse for telling me to sing a stupid Christmas song.

"Sing," she says again. And then the tears won't stop.

"Hold still," the doctor whispers.

I want to kick them for telling me it wouldn't hurt. It does. Five stitches. Tight, black thread. I feel every one of them go in and tug the broken skin back together. The doctor thinks he can just sew me up and it's all fixed. But it doesn't work that way. He cannot sew the giant hole in this day back together.

When we finally scramble back into my mom's blue car parked in the lot, she lights a cigarette, then slides a silver flask with her grandfather's initials out from underneath her seat.

"Why do you drink that stuff? It's bad for you, Mom," says Jamie. Jamie knows because he's tasted it before. He says it tastes worse than cough medicine.

"No, it's good for me on days like this. Believe me, it's god-damn good. Your dad is going to have a fit when he sees those stitches in Melissa's head."

I steal a sideways glance at my mom. I am looking for something in her face that tells me she is going to come back and stay with us, but I can't tell.

When we pull up alongside our house, Dad's waiting in the front yard for us. Jamie and Eden and I stay in the car as we watch our mom get out and stand in the driveway. As she talks to our dad, her body sways in the breeze and her eyes search the ground as if she's lost something. They start arguing.

"It wasn't my fault…"

"It's never your fault," he says. "Get out of the car, kids."

We don't move, terrified to make things worse.

My dad confronts her: "Have you been *drinking?*"

"No," she shouts. I get lost in the argument's details but remember the last thing Mom says to him: "*One* at a time. I can't do all three kids, you understand? If you want me to show up—then *one* at a time."

The skin on my head stings, expands, then feels like it might rip open any second.

I look at Eden and then at Jamie and then at myself in the small mirror. Eden is cranking his pinky finger into his ear, searching for wax. Jamie spits a loogie onto the sidewalk. I lift my hand to feel the knots of black thread.

One at a time. How will she decide which one of us to pick?

NOW

brown speckled hen

The sound of rain wakes me on my first morning at my mom's house in Olympia. It's not a hard or heavy downpour, but the kind of intermittent rain that sounds like someone is tapping at the window.

I pull on an oversized sweater I picked up at Goodwill and packed at the last minute. As I descend the stairs, I wonder if my mother will recognize me today or if I will ever hear her voice again.

Outside the kitchen window, I see my aunt tossing compost scraps to the chickens and ducks. They scramble over moldy fruit rinds, burnt toast, and bruised apples. My mom's husband, Kim, has brewed a pot of coffee and is already headed out the driveway with a truck full of Washington apples to be sold at the local farmers market. They married thirteen years ago. The wedding took place here in Olympia, out in their garden, when I was three weeks pregnant with my son Dominic.

Kim is the strong, silent type. Smart, kind, and able to conceal his emotions. The opposite of my father, who always wore his opinions and emotions on the tip of his Irish nose. Since my mom has been sick, I've witnessed Kim's affection for her. He stirs the cream and sugar into her coffee just the way she likes it. I've seen him enough over the past year and watched his large, callused hands feeding her spoonfuls of Cream of Wheat and gifting her with exquisite pieces of jewelry and tin boxes of licorice pastilles. I'm thankful for this.

Alone, I walk into my mom's room on the first floor and sit down next to her. I watch her breathe in and out as she sleeps. Her hands move slightly, rubbing the edge of a blanket between her fingers like babies sometimes do. Her fingers look as if they are dreaming.

I love her hands in this moment. They bring me back to the early days of standing over my newborn baby boy in complete awe. I would often put my fingers near his lips to make sure he was still breathing. I needed to be there every time he opened his eyes from a nap. If I heard a cry coming from his crib, I would sprint into his room certain he was filled with panic—panic and fear that his mother had abandoned him.

Whenever I went to the basement to fold laundry during his nap time, I couldn't stay more than a few minutes without running back upstairs to check on him. I had to be physically there as soon as he woke. I'd stand over his sleeping body, my hand on his chest, and assure him, "It's okay. I'm here. I'm here, sweet boy."

"I'm *here*," I whisper now to my mom as she sleeps.

A brown speckled hen from the yard suddenly trots through the open door of the bedroom, its yellow toenails clacking across the hardwood floor. It's one of the many chickens that roam the property. I stand up to open the door wider and shoo the hen out. But the chicken skids sideways against the television stand

and drops a gray and white splatter of shit at the foot of the bed. I try to corner the stray girl, but she starts flapping her clipped wings and crashes into the closet mirror.

My mom stirs, and I watch a genuine smile form across her dry lips. She's always loved to be surrounded by chickens. Me too.

THEN

big yellow house

We are moving to a new house in a new town. I'll be in kindergarten as soon as we get there. My dad tells me all about the house as he stuffs newspaper into the tall beer glasses from our kitchen cupboard. He tells me it's a giant farmhouse with a fenced-in pasture, a little barn, a plum tree, and an apple tree that grows golden and green apples.

"You won't believe it," he says, "but I rescued the house. The fire department was going to burn it down. They thought they could use it for a practice fire."

More than anything, I want to know what color the new house is. "It's a yellow house, a big yellow house," he tells me. That makes me smile. It's a perfect color for a new house.

Then he tells me something even better. "The house comes with chickens."

That night, I can't sleep because I keep thinking about the house that comes with chickens, and I have so many questions. I imagine chickens that are cream colored, black, and speckled. There must be red hens that lay warm brown eggs. There must be white roosters with bright red combs and yellow legs like pencils.

I wonder if they are tame, if I can pet their high tail feathers. I turn from side to side, over and over in my bed, until I can't stand it anymore.

I tiptoe down the hallway to my dad's room. I watch him through the crack of the door as he tosses his shirts and stretchy black socks into a cardboard box. His hair is a wild mess on top of his head. He and I both have the same type of curly hair that grows taller rather than longer. My dad picks up a can of beer from the top of a box and takes a long sip. He drinks a lot of beer lately. I know this because our garbage has been full of red-and-blue crumpled cans.

He catches me peeking at him from behind the door.

"Melissa," he says, "you're supposed to be in bed."

I tell him I can't sleep because I keep thinking about the chickens.

"It is way too late to be thinking about chickens."

As I stand in the doorway searching for words, my chin starts to shake. I don't want to cry but it's too late. I am like the red water balloon that burst open in my hands yesterday.

"What's going on?" my dad asks.

"Nothing," I say as I curl my toes into the thick shag carpet and straighten up my face.

He sets down his beer and looks at me, and I think he might be trying not to cry too.

"I was wondering if Mom has the directions to the house. I know she likes chickens. She always said so."

"Darlin'," he says. Then he stops and turns his face away from me and sighs. "Your mom's kind of doing her own thing right now. Remember?"

"Okay."

"Listen," he tells me, "your mom can come see you anytime she wants—wherever we live."

"But Jamie says she went far away."

"Not true," he says quickly.

I can tell he's mad at Jamie for spilling that secret by the way he says "Not true" in a hurry. I wonder if my dad even knows where she is. I wonder if he misses her as much as I do. I think he does.

My dad lifts me up and takes me to my bed. It helps when he gives me a back scratch and tells me more things about the big yellow house. He says the house is more than one hundred years old—that it has an attic big enough to live in, that it has room for a garden, and that we are going to plant corn and tomatoes and giant watermelons in the summertime. I hope Mom finds out about the yellow house that comes with chickens and decides to stay with us.

It takes forever to get to our new house. Finally we turn onto a bumpy dirt road.

"What's this place?" yells Jamie from the backseat.

"This is it," my dad says.

"We live on a dirt road?" asks Eden.

"Someday it will be paved," my dad responds.

Our car turns a corner, and there it is—a massive, old three-story farmhouse that is yellow just like my dad promised. I eye the enormous oak trees surrounding the house. Climbing trees, I think to myself. Trees to hang rope swings off, and trees to hide in.

Jamie, Eden, and I run up the steep stairs to see our new house. We race across the shiny linoleum and hardwood floors. The whole house echoes with the sounds of my brothers and me.

"Which one is my room?" shouts Eden.

"I get the top floor!" says Jamie and races toward the staircase.

Then we almost run smack into an old man sitting on the stairs. We all freeze. He has white hair and thick gray teeth.

"So you're the kids moving in, huh?" he says.

We stare at each other and then back at the creepy old man. Only Jamie is brave enough to speak. "Yeah."

"Where's your pop?"

"Uh, he's outside."

"Well, why don't you get him, because I've got a few more things to tell him about the place."

We scramble back down the stairs and tell Dad about the old man in the house.

"That's the owner. I mean the former owner, Mr. Bonner."

I follow my dad back into the house. Jamie and Eden run out to the biggest tree in the yard and start climbing.

My dad shakes hands with Mr. Bonner, who is still sitting on the steps.

"Listen up," the old man says to my dad. "I'm leaving you that white freezer. It's full of meat—there's a whole cow in there."

He looks down at the ground like he's talking to himself. "Should never have done it. I just couldn't take care of that cow after my wife passed. It was her pet. Thought it was the right thing to at least get the meat out of her. But it wasn't the right thing, after all. I won't go into details, 'cause I never believed in superstitious stuff before, but my wife has been letting me *know*."

"Well, is it a good cow? I mean, is it okay to eat?" asks my dad.

"It's good, all right. I don't know how to explain some things anymore, but I think it's best it goes with the house, like the chickens and all the white furniture."

My dad looks confused and says, "Why don't you go find those chickens, Melissa?"

Mr. Bonner grins at me with his gray teeth and says, "Go out around the barn. That's where they do their hanging out."

I'm out in the field in no time. It's hot, dry, and sweet smelling. The yellow grass brushes up over my ankles and I wish I hadn't worn my flip-flops. I could run faster across the field in my blue Keds.

The little barn in the center of the field leans to one side. It looks more like an old fort, but inside are bales of dusty hay, burlap sacks, empty nesting boxes, and cobwebs everywhere. I reach my hand into one of the sacks and pull out a handful of cracked corn. It's gritty and leaves a fine white powder on my palms. I think it must be the chicken food for sure, so I take a handful with me and walk around the other side of the barn. I hear cheep-cheeping sounds.

It's even better than I imagined. Not just chickens, but fuzzy baby chicks all in a row following their mother hen. Then I see a big red-and-black rooster coming my way. His tail feathers look black but shimmer green in the sunlight. I throw my handful of corn, scattering it in a fan all around me. The mother hen scratches at the ground, and all her little buff-colored chicks copy her. More chickens, white and black, come toward me, and soon I am surrounded by a giant horseshoe of chickens.

It is the best place in the whole world. Suddenly I feel like the little barn is also a new house, like this is a place that I am going to spend a lot of time. A strong, good feeling leaps into my chest.

I run across the field, back toward the big yellow house. I see Jamie and Eden climbing in a different tree, a tall oak with spiky leaves. I see my dad and old Mr. Bonner coming outside.

"Dad, Dad! I found baby chicks!"

Mr. Bonner looks down at the ground and shifts some dirt around with his shoe. "That's Mudder-Mudder," he says. "She's been here forever. Always has a flock of chicks following behind her. She'll take care of anything that comes along too. Once she took a wild duck under her wing. She's the best chicken here, and an Araucana, you know."

"What's an Araucana?" asks my dad.

"Lays colored eggs."

I think he's joking at first. There are such things as colored eggs? But he talks too seriously and slowly to be joking. He looks at me. "You take good care of Mudder-Mudder," he says.

We spend the whole day exploring our new house.

There's just one thing I'm not sure about. It's the whole cow in the white freezer. I'm trying to think how a cow could fit inside a freezer. The more I think about it, the more worried I feel about it. I stand in front of the freezer, which definitely seems too small for a cow. I tell Jamie about what Mr. Bonner said. How he froze his wife's pet cow and says he shouldn't have.

Jamie says, "That man was weird. I say we keep that freezer shut forever." I think that's a good idea.

Then Jamie jumps up from the floor and says, "Let's go find Mudder-Mudder and her chicks again."

I am right behind him, taking big steps like him. "Isn't this the greatest place we ever lived, Jamie?"

"I think it is. I think it is," he says.

And when Jamie says something twice in a row like that, I always believe him.

NOW

cherished

The speckled hen dashes out the back entrance of my mom's room and I push the heavy door closed behind her. This room is a mess. Orange plastic pill bottles, lip balm, and crumpled candy wrappers decorate my mother's bedside table. The dogs sleep on the bed, constantly shedding dander and black fur onto the blankets. Damp towels are strewn about, and socks hang over the backs of chairs like bats.

I want to clean it up but I don't feel like it's my place to do it. I don't want to offend my mom's husband, who seems to be doing all he can to keep her comfortable. Throughout the day, he enters and exits the room frequently with little to say. It feels like we are in a theater production and he and my aunt are the stagehands responsible for rearranging the set pieces. I am the understudy who showed up just in time for the final show.

As I look at the things this room holds, my head starts to hurt. I rub my left temple and eyebrow. I've been prone to severe headaches since I was a young girl. They hit me without warning and can linger for days. The pain has intensified over the years, sometimes so much that I want to detach my head from my body.

I'm well acquainted with the sharp, stabbing symptoms of an "ice pick headache" and the nausea that accompanies it. The migraine triggers are so varied that I've never been able to understand why they happen.

This time, though, I feel a wave of overwhelming anger bringing on the pressure in my head. My mom's room is a knick-knack shop filled with collected curios and crap. Up high in the window are colored bottles in blue, ruby red, and green. Netted glass balls from the sea, old slag-glass insulators, and a few tinted cordial glasses with delicate stems. A lavender Mason jar holds a hundred or so marbles—many of which she "borrowed" from my marble jar back at home on her occasional visits. The rickety bamboo shelf across from the bed is cluttered with an assortment of boxes and carved animal figures, as well as handfuls of jewelry, hair clips, and scattered Guatemalan worry dolls.

I sit looking at all of her treasures, searching for patterns and similarities between us. I don't have to look far—the hoarding gene runs deep. Even my father has lost control over the sheer amount of stuff he owns. He doesn't own a home anymore, but he pays rent on four buildings to house the antiques he buys and sells. He's become a hoarder of rare and exquisite things. I've talked to him about this affliction but he's stubborn. He knows that the "right buyer" will eventually come along and pay his price. Yet some of his pieces for sale have sat in the shop for more than twenty years. Sometimes I imagine him bent over like a contorted man, dragging every object and treasure he owns behind him. The parade of his possessions stretches for miles.

Likewise, my mother covets these "treasures" in her house. Why do I have the urge to smash every one? I want to take my arm and clear the shelves in a single swipe—hurl all her things out into the field where the spring grass will grow tall and hide them. Not one of these objects will keep her alive. Not one of them will take away the gnarled tumors from her liver—nor stop the ammonia from building up in her brain and destroying her brilliant mind.

What if I just did it? Smashed her beautiful things so that she could focus on what's important during her last days on this earth. If I were bold enough to take such an uncharacteristic action, perhaps she'd wake up and pay attention. I won't, though. I am still the silent, small girl hoping that my mother will come back.

And if I am honest with myself, I am a hypocrite. I too suffer this affliction of hanging on to things. I give value and meaning to ephemera and small objects. There are boxes of childhood treasures gingerly packed in our garage that I refuse to let go. A ball of tinfoil that a handsome boy threw at me in the seventh grade, a piece of driftwood named Elmo that I've held onto for thirty years, a collection of broken glass animals and earless horses. A set of seven metal jacks I used to play with. These are the things that I protected when my dad got into a huge financial mess. I despise this part of me that clings to the remnants of the past, and yet I often find myself holding on to them tightly.

In our yellow house, the antique I treasured most was the Good Fairy who lived up in my father's room. She was a small Victorian statue that he brought home from the flea market one year and placed on the windowsill above his bed. A foot tall and made of smooth white metal, she stood on her tiptoes with her slender arms open and outstretched toward the sky. She was young like me, caught in a moment of undeniable joy. Beneath her feet were the words "The Good Fairy." When I'd lie on my dad's bed and stare up at her, I felt just like her—like I could reach out beyond the borders of our yellow house. Like I could become anybody I wanted to be.

Sometimes when I looked up at her, she would tell me stories. Stories about the sparrow king, the black crows, and the storms and wars that were fought in the sky. The Good Fairy was a sure thing. And in our yellow house, things that were certain were the best—like the gravel rocks that led me down the driveway and back home from school each day, like the blackberry thicket, the pink tea roses, the marble collection in my room, and the five-hundred-year-old Chinese mud man sitting on his lacquer pedestal.

My mother, my father, and I hold onto things—we give them meaning in a world we cannot control. I wish I could sit next to my mom and just appreciate the beauty of each item in this room. Yet right now my mother's cherished objects feel untouchable to me. And though part of me feels an urgency to gather up as many pieces of her as I can before she leaves this world, I don't know what I'll do with these objects when she dies. Will they only remind me of her absence?

I remember that every year around Christmas, I waited and wondered when—and if—a present from her might arrive. It never did on Christmas Day or New Year's. By mid-January I always had given up hope. Then one February a giant package landed on our front porch.

THEN

merry to melissa

It arrives on a Saturday. A big box covered in brown paper with a dozen colorful stamps in one corner. Seconds later, I'm bolting up the stairs to my dad's room, skipping steps as I go.

"Dad, there's a giant box on the porch, and I think it's for us!" I yell.

He walks down the steps with me and eyes the package. "Looks like it's from your mother."

"Are you sure? Does it say her name on it somewhere?"

"Well, it's definitely her writing," he replies. "Maybe it's Christmas gifts."

I hold my breath, afraid to get too excited. I can't recall a box with my mom's handwriting ever arriving on our doorstep. "Oh, Dad, please can we open it now?"

"No, we need to wait for your brothers to get back home from the Conklins' house or wherever they took off to," he says as he lifts the box, sets it in the middle of the living-room floor, and hikes back up the attic stairs.

I sit down next to the package with a box of cheese crackers. I'm six and a half now and can read a little, but not when it's that fancy, curvy writing like my mom's. But I like the way it looks, thick black ink and all the letters wearing curly tails. I pull my knees up under my T-shirt and stretch it down under my toes.

With each square cracker I pop into my mouth, I think of what could be inside the box. My mind is wild with ideas: model horses, paint by numbers on velvet, cowgirl boots, a shiny lime-green purse, a stuffed white kitten made from real fur, a set of farm animals—so many possibilities! I finish the whole box of salty orange crackers, wondering if it could be an Easy-Bake Oven.

I lay my hands on the brown paper. I imagine my mom's hands pulling the paper tightly around the box. I can see her red garnet snake ring with the tiny diamond eyes coiled around her finger. I remember her hands full of rings, but it's her face I can't see clearly now.

I run out to the porch when I hear my brothers' voices in the yard.

"Jamie! Eden! Guess what? There's a huge box that came in the mail, and Dad says it's Christmas presents from Mom!"

"Since when does Mom send Christmas presents?" asks Jamie.

"She better have sent me a T-2 model rocket," says Eden.

"Dad, Dad!" I yell as I motion them in. "We can open the presents now!"

My dad makes a slice down the center of the box with his pocketknife. Inside the box is another box wrapped in bright, shiny pink paper. He hands that box to me and two smaller boxes to Eden and Jamie.

"How come Melissa gets the biggest one?" yells Eden.

"Biggest doesn't always mean the best," replies my dad.

I run my fingertips across the slick pink paper. There are old-fashioned angel stickers on one side and my mom's fancy writing on the other.

"What does it say, Dad?"

"Merry to Melissa," he reads.

I study the letters. Yes, I can see how it says that now. "Merry to Melissa."

I carefully tear the paper, saving the part with the angel stickers and the writing on it. The first thing I see inside the box are masses of yellow yarn. Grabbing onto the yarn, I pull out a tall and skinny handmade cloth doll. She is almost as tall as me, and I laugh. She has long yarn hair, two big, leather button eyes, and a smile embroidered in pink. She is as floppy as the scarecrow in *The Wizard of Oz* when he first meets Dorothy, and her long legs are thin like broomsticks. I hold her up and laugh again because even her head is floppy. I don't care—she's from my mom.

"I think your mom must have made this for you," my dad says, sounding unsure. "You ought to think of a name for her."

I stare at her sunny face.

"How about Jennifer?" my dad says.

"No, I need to think about it," I say.

I look over to see what my brothers got. Some kind of building-set things.

"What did Melissa get?" asks Jamie.

"Oh, some dumb old doll," says Eden.

I'm not much of a doll person, but I like how big and

floppy she is. I will introduce her to Bun-Bun, Monkey, and Bumble-Bear, and all the other animals in my room. I could even dress her in some of my clothes.

At school on Monday, I tell the most talkative girl in my class, Kat, about the doll that I got for a Christmas present from my mom. She asks me why my mom sent it in the mail instead of just putting it under the tree. I explain that I live with my dad and my brothers. "That's weird," she says. "Besides, Christmas happened two months ago, you know?"

Kat is a girl I want to be like. She is the smartest girl in class and talks a lot if she likes you. I try to think of something more to say. I want to be her friend.

"Her name is Merry," I say.

"Oh, I have a doll named Merry too," Kat says back.

"No. My mom, that's her name. Her name is Merry."

Kat just looks at me. I can tell she doesn't want to talk to me. Then she turns and runs toward the monkey bars.

I decide that Merry is a good name for my doll.

After dinner, I tell my dad about the name. I tell him that I am going to name her Merry, the same as Mom, since she made her. He looks at me almost the same way Kat did before she ran off to the monkey bars.

I push my spoon through the top layer of stretchy skin on the butterscotch pudding we're having for dessert. It's my favorite part. "Do you think Merry is a good name for her?"

My dad stares at me and doesn't say anything. He probably still thinks it should be Jennifer. Then he says, "Your mother's name is not Merry."

I have to think carefully. *What is he talking about?*

"Her name is Mikel. Your mom is Mikel," he says.

"But Dad, it said from Merry. Her name is Merry."

"No, it didn't," he says firmly. "Her name is Mikel."

I go into my room, close the door, and pull out the square of pink paper. I study it again: "Merry to Melissa." If that's not her name, then what does it mean? I feel like she tried to trick me. Why does she do that mysterious writing anyway? Does she even *know* how to sew a doll?

I lie down on my bed alongside the doll named Merry and try hugging her. But she is too thin and there is nothing to hang on to. I think how easy it would be to rip off her black button eyes. But that's not what I want. I just want to remember what my mom looks like. I can't recall how long it's been since her last visit when we got in the car accident and I had to get stitches and everything was ruined. I want to see her whole body at once, not just imagine her in pieces. I want to see her blue car and her blue eyes. I can see her long hair, but I can't remember how it feels. She is disappearing, fading away line by line like the invisible ink Eden got on his birthday.

I think of ways to make her come back. I could punch my fist through one of the windowpanes next to my bed. The noise would be satisfying and loud, and my hand might bleed. She might come if I had to get stitches again. She might come even quicker if I were in a hospital.

I lay my head against my doll's yellow yarn hair and pretend that it is my mom's hair alongside my face. I think I can smell her coffee and cigarette smoke. I shut my eyes. We talk about our favorite flowers. My mom tells me she likes red roses and orange tiger lilies. I tell her that I like buttercups, daisies, pink roses, and blue forget-me-nots. Maybe she would come if she knew how much I love flowers.

THEN

all kinds of flowers

When I turn seven, my dad lets me drop handfuls of tiny brown seeds into the earth outside the big yellow house. The soil in our garden is dark, strong smelling, and full of pale worms. I love the gritty feel of the dirt between my fingers. I drop my seeds carefully, one by one, even though my dad says to scatter them more quickly. He reminds me that some of them will sprout, but not all. I cover them cautiously so as not to upset the particular arrangement of my seeds.

For as long as I can remember, our garden has always been a vegetable garden. Every summer we have rows of corn, cucumbers, zucchini, red lettuce, and pole beans. This year, I have begged my dad to put in some flowers other than the same old yellow marigolds that are only planted to distract the bugs. He finally agreed and let me pick out five packets of flower seeds from the gardening store. I chose Shasta daisies, snapdragons, zinnias, impatiens, and blue forget-me-nots.

"Dad, where can we plant the flowers?"

He looks at the seed packets I have chosen and then looks around the garden for some open space. He squints in the sun as he reads the directions on the back of the flat packet. "Okay," he says. "Just so you know, some of these are annuals and some are perennials."

"What does that mean?" I ask.

He holds up two of the packets. "These are annuals. These won't come back once they bloom. They bloom once and then they die." I nod.

"These are perennials," he says, holding up the other packets. "These will come in the spring or summer—then go away and come back once a year."

I think about this.

"Sort of like Mom," I say, pushing the lettuce seeds down into dark soil. I keep my head down, afraid to see his face, but I can tell he's looking at me as I smooth out the dirt with my hands. The silence doesn't feel right.

"It's also like the lilacs," I say to break the quiet between us. "Those come back every Easter."

"Yes, like the lilacs," he says at last.

One year my mom came when the lilacs bloomed. Another time she came when the corn and lemon cucumbers were ripe. We never see her in the fall. Fall is back-to-school time. The garden begins to thin out, and the squash leaves turn yellow and crisp. We don't see her in December or at Christmas. The garden is always empty during those cold months.

As I lay out the seed packets on the ground in front of me, I also think about the wildflowers on our back hill—how every spring the bright, orange California poppies come back, as do the lupines, the bluebonnets, the buttercups, and the small purple ones that no one seems to know the name of. Now I know that my mom is the perennial type who visits and blooms once a year. When her petals begin to wilt, she hitchhikes out of town and we don't know when we will see her next. I want to tell her that someday I will bloom too.

NOW

mementos

Two days in, my mom is still unaware that I am here in Olympia—let alone in the room. She mumbles mixed-up phrases. She opens her eyes once and asks for a "lemon necklace," then falls back into a deep, medicated sleep.

I imagine Death circling around the house like a black crow, silent in its flight, noisy when it lands.

I sit on the stiff chair next to the bed and watch her eyes shift back and forth beneath her eyelids as if she is scanning the pages of a book. I wonder what she dreams about now. My phone vibrates, telling me I have a voice message from home.

I hold the speaker close to my ear and listen. "Hi, Mama. It's me, Bella. When are you coming back? I miss you…Ok-aaay, bye."

"I miss you too," I whisper.

There is no way I could have brought my family here. My excuse for going alone was that it would be too difficult for Bella and Dominic to see Grandma so ill. But that's not the whole truth. The reality is I don't want my children to see *me*. I am terrified that some hideous part of me could surface when my mom dies. I don't want to lose control of my carefully guarded self.

Besides, here at my mom's side, my job is to be a compassionate daughter, not a mother. I can't imagine tending to my children's needs right now. How would I nurture them when I am wrapped in my mother's death? Shouldn't I focus on being a better daughter to my mom during her last days?

She looks almost peaceful in her medicated state. I lift one of the curls away from her cheek and hold it between my fingers. It is as coarse as the garden twine my dad strung between the pole beans. I am seized by an urgent desire to steal a lock of her hair.

In the bathroom I find a pair of scissors stored in the medicine cabinet. I open the blades near my mother's cheek and snip the curl away from her. She flinches, as if she can feel the hair being taken—as if it's painful. But her eyes remain closed. I hold the curl, a capital C, between my fingers and quickly wish that I could put it back. Why do I feel I have to steal pieces of her?

I walk back upstairs with the curl and pick up the antique tin box that I gave my mom just last Christmas. This tarnished tin caught my eye immediately at the flea market. Small and unique boxes have always captured my attention. When I picked this one up, my breath caught at the sight of the letters MM embossed on the front, the initials my mom and I share.

Below the letters were the words "Christmas 1914" and a portrait of a young woman with her hair swept up. The seller explained the story behind the box. Seventeen-year-old Princess Mary of England commissioned nearly a thousand of these tins—packed with sweets, mementos, prayer cards, and cigarettes—to give as Christmas gifts to the soldiers fighting "the war to end all wars." I find comfort in objects that tell a story and resurrect a specific moment in history. I suppose that is why, like my father, I collect antiques. It didn't take but a moment to pull twenty-five dollars out of my wallet and buy the Christmas box for my mom.

As a child, when my mother showed up to see us, I took great pride in showing her the antique treasures in my room—my stamp collection, my glass animals, or the new marbles I had found. These were easy and safe things to share with her.

This family trait of collecting pieces of the past sometimes feels like a curse, or maybe just a distraction. But I can't let it go. Since my mom has not been able to part with anything throughout her illness, I will take Princess Mary's box home with me and find a place for it on my shelves full of memories. I move my fingertips over our shared initials on top of the tin, open the hinged lid, and place her curl inside. And suddenly I am back in my childhood room, seven or eight years old, surrounded by the treasures that provided a comfort and a steadiness I couldn't find elsewhere.

THEN

prized possessions

My dad stands in the doorway of my room, watching me as I rub an old dusting sock across the top of my dresser. I keep my back to him intentionally because I want to be by myself this morning and really hate it when he starts telling me *how* to clean my room. I know how to take care of my things.

"Whatcha up to?" my dad asks.

"Stuff," I say without turning. I pick the root beer–colored glass horse up off the dresser top and polish its smooth body with the sock.

"I was wondering…" He pauses. "I was wondering if you'd like to come down to the shop with me for a couple of hours." My dad rents a store now where he has a business stripping furniture and selling antiques. He transforms shabby old chairs, armoires, travel trunks, and writing desks into pieces of furniture fit for a queen.

I do love going to his shop, but not right now.

"No, that's okay," I say.

"We could go to Perry's Deli for lunch. Get a BLT?"

"No thanks, Dad. I just want to stay home today."

I ought to tell him that I already have my Saturday planned. I have a hundred knickknacks that need dusting and rearranging, and drawers out of order. I need to get out the pink Twinkle polish and shine the brass knobs on my bed too.

I continue to rub the root beer–colored glass horse, focusing on its delicate black hooves and the tiny bubbles trapped inside its see-through body. I silently chant to myself, *Go away, Dad. Go away, go away.* And not to be mean. I just want to be by myself in my room. This is the place where I can hear myself—a ticktock pulse inside me, the sureness of my footsteps across the floor. Here in my room, I allow myself to time travel and even become other girls if I need to. Here I become the grand-prize winner in the International Room Cleaning Competition, my own private game in my own private world.

The IRCC is a very specific contest in room cleaning and, most importantly, design. The IRCC judges arrive wearing navy-blue suits. They carry clipboards with thick pads of yellow paper. They are immediately impressed with how I have so carefully arranged the things in my room. The striped bed quilt is stretched flat without a single crease. The window ledge is slick with Old English furniture polish—and each freshly polished brass knob on my bed practically winks at them.

I hear the judges chat among themselves as they point to my glass animal collection. They like that I have allowed the wild glass tigers to mingle with the domestic fan-tailed birds. They turn and admire the old chandelier crystal that hangs on clear fishing line in the window and makes a thousand rainbow prisms dance around the room when the afternoon sun comes in. They peer into the glass cabinet that holds many of my most valuable knickknacks. They give me high marks on attention to detail and arrangement.

One of the judges asks me to show them my most prized possession.

"There are so many," I say. I look around, trying to remember what I showed them last time. I want to show them something they haven't seen before.

I open the lid of the leather box that belonged to my grandma Rita and take out a small red bean no bigger than one of my molars. I hold it up for the judges to examine. Attached to the top of the bean is a tiny rice-colored elephant. I carefully tug at the little carved elephant and the top of the bean comes off—revealing that it is hollow inside. Now comes the best part: I turn the bean upside down and spill into my palm seven of the teeniest elephants imaginable—all the color of rice and as small as typed letters. They lay flat, like sprinkled confetti in my hand. The judges nod their heads in approval over this herd of elephants living inside a hollow red bean.

"Show us more," they say.

I feel certain that today is a perfect day to win another room-cleaning competition.

"Please..." I hear my dad say faintly. His voice is a whisper, a feather floating across the room toward me.

I turn to my dad framed in the doorway. There are tears in his eyes.

"Please? I need you to come with me."

I feel something run up my spine and nestle itself underneath my hair. I touch the back of my head where it tingles.

"What's wrong, Dad?"

"I just don't want to be alone today. Please?"

The tears change everything. I don't know how to respond.

I stare back down at my glass horse, suddenly wishing I could throw it against the hard surface of the floor and shatter it into jagged pieces. But as much as I want to break something, I can't. Just like Jamie says, I am a "chicken girl."

Sometimes I want to be like Jamie. I want to know how it feels to throw glass bottles in street gutters, hurl eggs at Mr. Rivasplata's car, steal salami from the grocery store, hear the sound of my fist breaking through Sheetrock, and dodge the Novato police. But I can't. I'm the good one, the quiet one, the one who never gets into trouble. A skinny toothpick holding up the whole house. I am the one my dad counts on.

My carefully planned day slips away. I set the glass horse down and slide it across my dresser like I am making a well-thought-out move on a chessboard. I push its front hooves to the edge of the dresser and there it halts.

"It's okay, Dad. I'll go with you."

"Thanks, darling."

As I lace my shoes, I think about my dad's tears and the night he came home and told us his mom had died. I had so many questions about how she died but my dad wouldn't say. Jamie and Eden hadn't spent a lot of time with Grandma Rita, but I had. A year or two ago, my dad put me on a plane and I flew by myself from California to LaGuardia Airport to visit her. A driver picked me up to take me to her house in a town called Katonah.

Grandma Rita was in bed when I arrived. After I gave her a hug, she told me she'd always wished for a little girl but she only had sons. I sat beside her and we talked for a bit. Or rather she asked me lots of questions. I was terribly shy. I had so many thoughts that I couldn't get out of my mouth: What was I going to do while I was here? Why hadn't my brothers come? Why was she staying in bed? Where was I going to sleep?

I spent that night in the upstairs room, listening to the sound of the cicadas and the attic window rattling. What I remember most vividly about my visit is peering into her dining-room cabinet filled with beautiful china and glass objects. A red swan, hand-painted plates, and an ornate emerald egg perched on a gold stand.

When Grandma Rita died, my dad's tears startled me but they made sense. He was going to miss his mother. I'm guessing that my dad is upset now because his girlfriend broke up with him a few days ago. He's had a lot of girlfriends, but he never picks the marrying kind. Usually they are much younger than him and not interested in having three instant kids. Not that we're interested in a young mom who's not our mom anyway.

When my dad has a steady girlfriend, I feel like I can take a huge, deep breath and slip away from always having to pay attention, always trying to keep the peace. I hate being the only girl in a house of boys.

On the way to his antique shop, we stop at Perry's Deli and buy two Pepsis and BLTs.

My dad's shop is packed with antique furniture angled in every direction. I walk through the maze of desks, dressers, tables, cabinets, armoires, old-fashioned barber chairs with red velvet upholstery, and shelves full of green and pink Depression glass. The antique medical cabinets have thirty-five skinny oak drawers in different sizes made for doctors' scalpels and tools.

I could hide a lot of treasures in a cabinet like this. I'd love to show it to the judges of the room competition.

But I can tell that I'm going miss out on the International Room Cleaning Competition, and the IRCC judges are going to pick someone else to win the grand prize today. I'm not certain when my mom will come next, but when she does, I'm going to make sure that my room is the best and most interesting place she's ever seen. She's going to be amazed—just like the judges of the IRCC.

NOW

between paper and pen

My aunt Joanna taps on the bedroom door. "I'm going into town for an hour or so. Do you want to come with? You might find a treasure at a post-Christmas sale to bring back to the kids." She's right. I'll need to bring something back to Bella and Dominic. But I can't focus on that right now.

"I think I'll stay here," I say.

"You doing okay?"

"Yeah. So-so."

"It's just hard, isn't it? There's not a lot we can do, except be here with her."

I nod. "I'd feel better just staying here." She smiles in a way that tells me she understands. I watch from the upstairs window as she starts the car and drives down the gravel road.

I'm glad for time alone. It's deeply wired in me. The long stretches of time that I spent in my room as a young girl balanced me. In my room, the world felt small and manageable. Whenever the shouting between my dad and brothers escalated, I had a place to hide. And when Eden and Jamie fought after school (which seemed like every day), the pitch of Eden's piercing screams kept me in my room where I was safe. Jamie always preyed on Eden in the absence of adult supervision until he cried out "Mercy." I felt sorry for Eden but I didn't know how to protect him.

As a mother now, I struggle to find a similar kind of solitude—and I desperately need it. I'd be more balanced, more patient, less stressed out with my children and husband if I gave myself a time-out in a room of my own. But I can't just say, "Hey kids, I need to go spend a couple hours—or a day—alone in my room."

Whenever I can, I steal stretches of time to be by myself. When my children were younger, I'd sometimes strap them into their car seats at night and drive until I could hear the silence of them sleeping. If they didn't fall asleep right away, I'd turn up the radio to quell the anger percolating inside me. I was tired and desperate for time to think, to be, to breathe by myself for a minute. In those moments, I couldn't help but resent my mom even more, imagining her driving off alone to wherever she wanted to travel after she left us, never having to think twice about anyone but herself.

Before I left home to come here to Olympia, I came across notes I'd scrawled in journals. These were thoughts that I intended to keep to myself.

Mom,

There are times I wish I could flee too. Even when the kids are their worst, I do not strike them. I never will. As I carried Dominic's tired and angry body up the stairs tonight, I felt the heaviness of love. This is the burden I choose. You know,

Mom, you did not do the same. You left—you took the easy road out. I wish I could trust you. Sometimes I wish I had that mom—someone I could have curled up next to and felt completely safe.

Now, finally alone in the upstairs office bedroom, I sit and pull open the bottom drawer of my mom's metal filing cabinet. Inside a manila folder, I discover a colored-pencil drawing that is without a doubt my brother Jamie's work. It is an intricately drawn fish, a marlin I believe, with the word "MOM" woven into its black and blue scales. Jamie is the artistic one; he's never been able to stop drawing. That's what he did on the borders of his seventh-grade math homework papers instead of solving the problems and on every small scrap of paper he found in the house. The backs of the PG&E bills and the phone bills were covered with red-and-black ink-pen drawings. He even drew on the unfinished Sheetrock in his bedroom closet.

Much of what he chose to draw was strange. Creatures that were half-fish, half-men. Devil faces with distorted tongues and foreheads. Arms floating in the sea. Fish with sharp, vicious teeth. Men with scars all over their bodies. Hearts, bleeding or struck by lightning. But sometimes what he drew was beautiful. A rainbow trout jumping out of calm waters. A fish swimming inside another fish. Or this marlin decorated with a hundred shimmering scales. But Jamie didn't always like his drawings. He'd get mad and crumple them up or turn something nice into a screaming man with needles sticking out of his body.

I was jealous of how well Jamie could draw. I could only manage to draw flowers and stick people. Eden couldn't have cared less about Jamie's drawings. He was more interested in building model rockets and dissecting old circuit boards and CB radios. I remember my dad telling Jamie he was going to flunk out of school if he didn't shape up and stop goofing off with his doodling. But Jamie was so good with a pen that he could change his grades from Fs to Bs on his report card (at least until the parent-teacher conferences came up and my dad discovered the truth).

Regardless of what my father believed, Jamie had a gift. Once I asked him if he ever wanted to go to art school. He shrugged and said, "I don't want to go to any kind of stupid school. I just like to draw."

As bizarre as some of his drawings were, something pulled me toward them and made me want to touch them. I kept a collection of Jamie's drawings hidden in my room. I'd find them crumpled up in the wastebasket and would smooth them flat and save them. I'd study them sometimes when I was alone because I was convinced there was a secret about Jamie hidden in his drawings. Between the dark ink lines and the scales of fish, there were stories he was trying to tell.

I'm worried about my brother. Beneath all his tattoos, I see the lost little boy he became so early in his life. I see the self-doubt he faces every day and the demons he wrestles endlessly.

Jamie is like me. Our early memories are as vivid and detailed as the lines on our palms. We both know how to don a beaming smile and say everything is okay, when we really mean "Everything is shit."

I called him before I flew here to Olympia. He said there was no way he could leave his family or afford a plane ticket from Hawaii, where he lives now painting houses. But clearly he also couldn't handle seeing her so sick. As a kid, Jamie used to say that when Mom got old and gray, he was going to be the one to take care of her. I think he really wanted that. But he's having a hard time taking care of himself right now. Halfway through our phone conversation, I heard an odd raspy noise that sounded like the deep inhalation someone makes when smoking marijuana.

"Are you smoking a joint or something?" I asked him.

Then I realized he's not smoking, he's sobbing.

I felt foolish for asking such an insensitive question. I know exactly what he's feeling as he attempts to hold it all in. All the grief and guilt over what is happening, and our utter lack of control over it. "I'm so sorry, Jamie."

"Why does she have to die?" he asked. The simplicity and childlike quality of his question stunned me.

"I don't know, Jamie. But it's all going to be okay," I lied.

Sitting here looking at my brother's drawing for my mom, I begin to cry. Not for Mom, but for Jamie's loss. He is the artist and the fisherman. He is my brother who could fall apart any day, my brother who always believed that *he* was the reason our mother left. There is no word, no bandage big enough for the size of his wound.

———

A photograph falls out of the second folder I've pulled from my mom's filing cabinet. I've seen this picture before. It's my mom in the West Indies. She's all of twenty-two or twenty-three years old. Several more photographs show her smiling in a blue swimsuit. The light in these photographs has a dreamlike quality—washed out, blue green, and slightly overexposed, making them seem like they are from some other part of the world where the light reflects off the ocean differently. In one of the photographs, a chocolate-skinned woman is standing next to Mom, holding a tray topped with a drink that has a pink umbrella sticking out over the rim.

I recognize this photo because my mother had it out during one of my visits a little over a year ago. I inquired about it because I couldn't comprehend how she had ended up in the West Indies, of all places, when she had three small children at home. When she was on her second glass of wine, I felt bold enough to ask her. Even though her health was starting to fail, I didn't try to stop her from drinking because I wanted the straight story, unblemished and from her mouth.

"My parents sent me there," she said.

"For how long?"

"A month."

"Why?"

"Because they didn't know what else to do, I guess. They were worried that I was going to have some kind of breakdown."

I didn't say anything, sensing that I have caught her in a rare moment of revealing something about herself.

"They sent me to this very upscale resort so that I could have some time to think and figure out what I was going to do with myself. I was *not* well. I was having a hard time being a decent wife and a mother, and I needed to get away."

She walked to the stove and clicked the burner until it lit up with a blue and orange flame. Then she held a cigarette against the fire 'til it caught and lifted it to her lips.

"So my parents came up with this ludicrous plan. My father dragged me down to a New York lawyer—a real stuffed shirt—and told me what was going to happen. After a week of being at the resort, the lawyer said all I needed to do was write a letter to your dad, begging him to come get me off the island. If I wrote a letter and your dad refused to come get me—which the lawyer assured me that your dad would do, since he had his job and you three kids to take care of—that could stand as grounds for me to divorce him and get custody of you kids."

She stopped talking like she was suddenly caught back in that moment.

"It was god-awful sitting in that office wedged between my father and that slick lawyer. He looked at me like I was white trash and told me I was lucky because he would sort it all out for me."

"But you ended up staying at the resort for a month, right? Dad never came to get you?"

"That's right."

I was trying to imagine my mom there, lonely in her blue swimsuit, weighing all her choices. "So what did you do there all that time?"

"I partied."

"You *what?*"

"I partied," she confirmed.

I don't know why her answer startled me, but it did. I wanted a different explanation, even if it was a lie. I wanted her to say that she thought about us the whole time or that it was one of the most difficult periods of her life. I wanted her to sit down on that kitchen chair and tell me for once that she was sorry for what happened.

"I'm tired, darlin'—I gotta head to bed," she said, throwing back the last sip of wine.

But I have one more question. "What about the letter? Did you ever send the letter to Dad?"

"No, I just couldn't do it. It was all so ridiculous." She shrugged.

I watched her sway out of the room.

And that's when I understood the layers beneath her words. She didn't send the letter because it would have meant she was committed to coming back to us. And she wasn't. She needed the vacation but she didn't want custody of us.

The photograph of my mom in the West Indies looks different now that I take a second look at it. The ocean light is dirty, and my mom's smile and the drink with the pink umbrella are both empty. There is a quiet hum inside me, a familiar feeling of standing alone in a house and waiting for someone or something to walk back through the door.

THEN

terry, our ninth live-in

We've gone through at least eight live-ins since our mom left. They come and go like stray cats that show up on the porch of our yellow house and then move on. Sometimes they say we are more like wild animals than children. Jamie and Eden are often sent home from school—when they aren't ditching. There are broken bones, burned skin, fistfights, and fires to contend with while looking after us.

Right now, we have Terry. She's our ninth. She tells me ghost stories. Not the make-believe kind, but the true kind—stories of her real-life personal encounters with ghosts. She said that she felt the presence of a ghost in our house the first time she stepped into my dad's attic bedroom, but she took the job as a live-in anyway because she sensed that it was a *good* spirit. I like the idea of good spirit living in our house.

Terry is a grandma type who dyes her hair bright orange and layers her whole face with powder as thick and white as the Duncan Hines cake mix we used to eat beneath our old house. She's got eyes that crinkle up when she smiles, and she smells like roses.

One day, she sits me down at the dining-room table with a handful of pretzels and says, "Honey, you need to know the truth about ghosts."

"Okay," I say.

She raises her red eyebrows to the top of her forehead, stares into my eyes, and tells me the true story about the time she came home to find a lit cigarette smoking itself over her bed.

"There it was, puffing and smoking and waving up and down without a person attached to it. I knew right away that my mother was smoking that cigarette. It had a tiny stain of Coral Reef right on the tip, and that was *her* lipstick. She wore that coral even though it was too much orange for her pale skin. You see, she had been denied cigarettes during the last days of her life while lying on her deathbed. You've got to understand something about spirits, my dear Melissa. They show up to *tell* you things. And my mother was telling me that she would not be denied her smokes, even in the afterlife. So there she rested on my own bed that day, smoking the life right out of that cigarette."

I lick all the sandy salt off the last pretzel.

"God bless her, she was stubborn," Terry continues. "I never touched one of those deadly sticks, and I'll tell you something else. I'm going straight to heaven because I have seen enough ghosts in my life and I don't want to end up in their gang."

When Terry stops talking, I don't ask her what happened next. I think for a long time about that cigarette floating in the air with its lipstick tip.

A few days later, Terry takes me with her to do our grocery shopping. I count stop signs as we drive and wonder if she's going

to let me pick out a root beer at the market. I am still embarrassed about peeing in the back of our station wagon on the last
trip to the Mayfair market. I kept saying I had to go, but Jamie
and Eden were fighting and yelling so much that Terry couldn't
hear me.

We pass stop sign number four, and Terry suddenly hits the
brakes hard and pulls over to the side of the road. The wagon
swerves back and forth, tossing me against the door.

"My God, did you see that!" she exclaims. She makes a
U-turn in the middle of Novato Boulevard and pulls into the
dusty corner lot where the town nativity scene is set up every
Christmas. Today, a dozen paintings in fancy frames are propped
up against wood crates.

"Would you look at that," she says, transfixed. She stares out
the window at a painting directly in front of us. The dust around
the car clears, revealing a large oil painting of an ocean sunset
with turquoise waves and an orange sky.

"That is beauty on a canvas," she says slowly. "It's the most
truthful thing I have seen in a long time."

"*That?*" I ask.

"Yes, that," she says.

"It's nice," I say to be polite.

She jumps out of the car, walks over to the painting, and
stands there with her orange hair waving in the wind and
blending into the painted sunset. A man in a wide-brimmed
straw hat steps out of an old green pickup truck and approaches
her. He seems to be trying to make eye contact with her, but her
eyes do not leave the painting. I stay in the front seat, sticking
my finger into the old yellow foam beneath the cracked leather,

and I think, *I don't get it. It's a picture of waves.* I look for an answer in the other paintings. More waves and beaches. More orange sunsets.

She hurries back to the car and wiggles into the seat behind the steering wheel.

"I've got to have that painting. We're skipping the grocery store, sweetie. I've got to see what I have left in my bank account."

"Does it cost a lot?" I ask.

"The artist will give me a good price if I have cash."

Then I see the desperation in her face, her mind calculating and wondering how she can get the money. I've seen my dad with this look when he's talking about the bills he can't pay. I figure the painting must cost more than a hundred dollars. Maybe a thousand.

"Have you ever seen such beauty, sweetie pie? Such godliness?"

I turn my head to her. The powder on her cheeks has turned thick and pasty from the tears running down her face.

"It's very nice," I say, afraid to admit I don't understand what she's talking about.

"I think that's what heaven must look like. I'm almost certain of it," she says as if she is talking to herself.

Terry emptied out her savings from the bank to buy that painting. She brought it back to our house wrapped in brown paper and placed it safely on the floor behind her bed board.

Two weeks later she dropped the news just like all the others had. I wasn't that surprised because she had been acting different ever since the day of the painting. She didn't have time to tell any ghost stories, and she seemed to be in hurry about everything. She told my dad that she'd found an apartment across town to live in on her own. My dad offered to pay her more money but she said it wasn't about the money.

"Is it something to do with the painting?" I asked her before she left.

She smiled at me with her crinkly eyes and said, "It's sort of about that painting, sweetie."

I waited for her to say something more but she didn't.

The painting of the ocean put a spell on her, and I couldn't understand why. How could a stupid painting change someone's mind about living with us? I tried to tell my dad about this but he didn't get it. He said that maybe Terry just needed her own space and that it was a lot of work for someone her age to take care of three kids all day.

My dad is looking for a live-in that can stick around a little longer this time. He's got a classified ad in the *Novato Advance* that comes out on Saturday. I ask him when Mom can come back to visit. My dad replies that he hasn't been able to reach her and that maybe she has moved to a new house again.

I keep trying to picture the places she lives. Sometimes I think I can see her sitting at a sunny kitchen table where she drinks coffee with cream and sugar. The curtains behind her are yellow with tiny white flowers, and her ashtray is a ruby-colored glass heart. My imagination is all I have. *It's okay*, I tell myself. Maybe she will call soon. Maybe she will come and be our new live-in.

NOW

into the wild, blue yonder

From afar, my mom was aware of the ever-changing hands in our house. But she never indicated if it bothered her. The idea of that is unfathomable to me; I can't imagine someone else raising my children. When Dominic and Bella were younger we'd frequent the local parks. They loved digging in the sand, climbing the giant spider, and swinging from the monkey bars. But the park was one of the most lonely and isolating outings for me. I couldn't help noticing the children that were there with nannies. Even if the nannies were attentive, I'd focus on the kids who were barefoot and sitting in the sandbox with vacant eyes—certain they were sad and wishing for their parent to be there with them.

My father continued to find an eclectic assortment of live-ins to look after us: couples, hippies, grandmothers, drill sergeant types, cat ladies, and psychics.

Gerta, the Olympic swimmer from Germany, was one of the first. I liked her because she saved me from drowning in the undertow at Stinson Beach. Dorothy from Bakersfield carried around a little dog named Toto. (Yes, really.)

Sonny and Wes were teenage neighborhood boys who

occasionally watched us in between live-ins. They entertained us by lighting matches and setting off firecrackers in the house. But after the living-room curtains caught fire, my dad didn't ask them back.

Then there was Lynn with the emerald-green eyes and Tia with the blue eye shadow. Jennifer, who said she could teach cats to talk like humans. And Claire and Arthur, who taught us the importance of the peace sign. And then Ken and Sharon, who left without saying as much as good-bye to any of us (and were creepy anyway).

Our live-ins often seemed to pack their bags and leave on short notice. Taking care of three feral kids full-time couldn't have been an easy job. Still, we imagined our mother might come back. Every day we fought to understand our place in the world and wondered who the next set of players in our yellow house might be.

I keep perusing my mother's files, searching for any sort of clue to better understand her. My fingers graze a manila folder stuffed down in the back of the cabinet. I pull it out and see my mom's handwriting penciled across the top:

Letters Never Sent & Thought Dabbles

The folder feels heavy in my hands. Letters *never sent?* I open it slightly, enough to catch a glimpse of folded-up letters and torn sheets of perforated paper and the scent of my mother's hands, metallic from her fingers full of rings. Why would she keep a file of letters that went unsent? What has she kept hidden? I close the folder, questioning the integrity of snooping through her personal things. But I'm desperate for something to hold on to.

I shut my eyes and sit with the folder on my lap, wanting to do the right thing although everything feels wrong. What if there is something in here that I am not supposed to know? A tremor creeps into my hands and then consumes my whole body.

I open my eyes, reach into the folder, and draw out a letter written on hotel stationery to my great-grandmother. "The Fairmont Hotel and Tower—Atop Nob Hill in San Francisco" is embossed across the top in blue and gold letters.

Dearest Gran,

I can't begin to express all that has happened to me since I last wrote. The European plans had to be scotched for a while— Daddy didn't approve and I didn't feel I had enough money. He still doesn't approve, and I still don't feel totally financed, but I'm going anyway. It may sound foolish, Gran, but I think this may be my Rubicon. I am absolutely terrified about the whole venture, but by dammy, I'm going to overcome the fear and GO. Karen and I will go to Paris where a friend has an apartment. Then down through France into Spain, up into Italy, across Greece, and down into the islands. From there things get a bit hazy—perhaps Switzerland and Germany. I would like to stay until December and then come home for

Christmas. There is a possibility of J. taking the babies to NY then. Well, I refuse to spend Christmas without my tads. Gran, I can hardly wait to see the Parthenon by moonlight. And Knossos will rebloom with the Minoan culture while we are there. Be prepared for adventure!

I am aware that my mom traveled to Greece sometime after she left us. I have gathered that from things my dad said in passing and photographs I glimpsed of her on the Aegean Sea with her roommate Karen, whom she mentions here in the letter. But I don't think she ever made it back to us "tads" that Christmas.

I remember my mom once telling me about her Gran and how close they were. I wonder why she never sent off this letter—and why she's kept it all these years.

I pull out another letter, addressed to her sister.

Dearest Joanna,

I am in limbo rather. Can't quite get it together. I'm floating between Novato and Stuart's and the city and feeling pretty lost. Fuck, I'm so uncertain—school? Teepee? Nepal with Stuart for three magic months? Back with the kids? Help! Too many choices. I want to escape to the woods most of all but I am so unsure of making it. The woods, the woods, the wonderful woods—woulds? Tomorrow I'm back, wonder if I should. No permanence is necessary, however—dear Obadiah. Are we children caught in the universal turmoil, or is the wood just wet and low? To have the good fortune to have

so many opportunities is misfortune for me. I wish I had my
sweet blue Car to help me decide—him being my best friend
and all.

I close my eyes and watch my mom drive away in her "sweet
blue Car." Where did she flee to when she left? And if she
wanted opportunity so much, why did she call it a misfortune?
The chronology of her life after abandoning us has always been
unclear to me. Even my father was uncertain as to her where-
abouts much of the time—especially during the first few years
after she disappeared and left him trying to pin her down for
answers.

I continue reading.

Off to the wild, blue yonder. Canada can't be so cold in
September. I'm not deserting and shirking all responsibility.
I'll probably go to Florida actually—if I bus it, then I will have
lots of time for thought and call my Gran at the same time.

I'm not sure how to react to my mom's carefree musings
about "where to go next" that blithely disregard her responsibilities. Maybe I should be outraged, but I'm not. I'm fascinated.
Maybe I'm even jealous. Somewhere deep inside me, I can relate
to my mother's irrepressible desire to be free of everyone, everything. Maybe I have inherited this fleeting nature too. Though
I love my children passionately, I leap at opportunities for time
away from them.

It's not a lack of love but a fierce desire to be alone. I need
it often, this solitude, this time to think and figure things out.

And it never feels like enough. At other times I wish I could disappear and come back as a new and improved mother—a top-of-the-line, high-efficiency model. Maybe that was my mom's intention at one point, but it never materialized. Or maybe she feared she would never be anything more than a mother in life.

When I was standing in line at the dreaded dollar store several years ago, with an armful of cleaning supplies and cheap plastic containers, my daughter Bella blurted out a statement that caught me off guard and silenced me. She said, "Mama, how come you never wanted to be anything when you grew up?"

I was crushed by her perception of me. Was I just a mother and nothing else in her eyes?

The truth is, I never imagined being a mother. Growing up, I didn't have it on my list of dreams. For a long time, I wanted to be an actress. Later, I dreamed of traveling as a photographer for *National Geographic* or going on archaeological digs where I would discover lost treasures and ancient artifacts. I was also certain that someday I'd ride on the Olympic equestrian team and have my own stable of horses. But it never occurred to me that I would follow in my mom's footsteps and become a mother.

That familiar fear starts rattling around inside me again: what if a leaving tendency lies dormant inside me? Nobody believes me when I say this, but they don't know how quickly lives can get derailed, how maybe my mom didn't want to leave, or intended to leave only for a little while that became forever.

Then another thought shakes me: my brothers and I share a common history of longing for our mother, and I can't help but wonder if all three of us may have made the same monumental mistake. Perhaps, in our silence after her departure, we gave her permission to leave. Maybe we unintentionally handed our mom three free tickets to travel the world with little or no guilt about the family she'd left behind. Maybe we handed her the orange Monopoly card that said "Get out of jail free anytime."

Perhaps she was just testing the bounds of our love when she left, and we failed her. We waited for her to change her mind, but we didn't fight for her or plead for her to come back. And even when she visited occasionally, we still never begged her to come back and stay for good. We were so awed to see her again in person that we never thought to ask for more, to try to win her back.

Maybe she needed someone to fight for her. Maybe she needed my dad to hold onto her and tell her she was good inside and out when she had thoughts of leaving us. And when she walked out the front door, maybe she needed us to grab onto her waist or wrap ourselves around her and beg her not to go. Maybe she was planning to come back but no one asked her.

So what did we do instead? Jamie, Eden, and I sat and waited on our porch steps on hot summer evenings while mosquitoes buzzed and bit our ankles and elbows. We went to the Marin County Fair, sunk our teeth into caramel apples, rode the Ferris wheel high up in the sky, and wished she was there with us. I hid under my yellow and green quilt with Bun-Bun at night and waited. I sat on the hay bales stacked high in the barn and wondered when we would see her next. I lay down alongside my hamster Fuzzy's grave on our hillside with handfuls of yellow buttercups, and waited.

We were always waiting.

I stop reading her dabbles and letters because I am afraid.

What if her letters trigger something unpredictable inside of me? Like my mom, I could go off track. What makes me immune from retreating to the woods or skipping out the front door into the wild, blue yonder?

NOW

transparent

I sit across from my aunt Joanna and Kim at the dinner table while my mom continues to sleep and dream in the next room. The house is quiet and heavy. We've ordered Mexican food from the local diner, and Kim sets out a six-pack of Corona and lime wedges. We're sitting around the table making conversation but I'm not really present—maybe none of us are.

My thoughts keep sliding into the undeniable truth: *she is dying.* The sentence plays over and over like a recording that can't move forward. I want to retreat upstairs to be alone and read more of her letters. But I'm also afraid to read them all at once. I suppose a kind of measured self-control defines my nature. Similar to the way that I never finish some of my favorite books—because I don't want the story to end and I don't want the characters to leave me.

My aunt sets down a plate of leftover green-and-red Christmas cookies. It's odd to be celebrating this holiday under the same roof as my mother, since growing up, we rarely saw her at Christmas. I excuse myself to make a call home. Bella answers.

"When are you coming back?" is her first question.

"I'm sorry, Bella. I don't know yet."

"So you're missing our whole Christmas vacation?" Bella sews stitches of guilt like a master seamstress.

"Are you having some get-togethers with your friends?" I ask, trying to distract her.

"They all have *family* plans."

I hear my husband in the background. "Don't make Mommy feel bad, Bella."

I'm grateful that Anthony is with the kids while I'm here. He doesn't spend nearly as much time with them as I do, and sometimes I feel resentful that he gets to be the dad who steps in just in time for the fun activities. As a single parent raising three children, my dad was always crazy-busy and running to catch up. He was the role model I had for a parent, and what I learned from him is that one parent can do it all. Thus, I tend not to ask for help when I could use it, which is not the best recipe for balance in our family.

I've been vague with Bella about the things going on with my mom. Maybe if I allowed my emotional ups and downs to be seen, she would be easier on me.

"I'm bringing you a present back from Washington," I tell her. Which is a lie only in that I haven't actually bought anything yet. But whenever I'm gone for more than a day, I always return with a gift to soften my absence. This trip to Olympia may prove to be the longest I have ever been away from my children.

Several years ago, when I traveled to the desert for three days, Bella was furious by the time I returned. One of the reasons that my absence was especially upsetting was because Daddy couldn't help with her hair. I was the one who combed out the knots each morning, fashioned ponytails, and snapped in the colorful barrettes. I knew from personal experience that fathers do not have a great deal of skill with long and tangled hair.

When I returned and walked through the front door, Bella looked at me with a stern face and said, "I almost forgot you were part of this family."

Her extravagant comment left me speechless. Who was this spirited little girl of mine who wasn't afraid to say or show what she felt? Dominic had never challenged me in quite the same ways, and I wondered if Bella was sensing my mothering insecurities or reading the tea leaves on the bottom of my cup.

"It sounds like you missed me a lot when I was gone," I finally replied.

She burst into tears. As I held her and felt her sobs, heavy against my chest, I was grateful to comfort my little girl who missed me. I also became aware of the physical contact I must have longed for from my mother as a child.

I talk with my family a bit more and then finally hang up, still thinking about Bella's frustrations over my occasional absences. On a deep level, I understand her strong reactions. As a mother, I make an effort to be a better parent. I buy self-help and parenting books and subscribe to *Family Circle* and *Parenting* magazines. I'm trying to find my way, but sometimes I feel the weight of all my shortcomings at once. I am not always a good mother, and there are days where I am humorless, judgmental, curt, and preoccupied. I try not to let myself get defeated by the daily grind of motherhood, but sometimes I feel locked in the nightmare of domesticity.

When I interact with other mothers on the school yard, I feel transparent. I don't want to talk about domestic details like sleep schedules, Swiffers, standardized testing, or where to buy discounted organic produce and Disneyland tickets. Really, that sort of discussion shouldn't get to me, but it does. I know that it's part of being a parent—sharing resources and all that. But sometimes I want to run when I see these well-organized mothers walking my way. I can't take in any more information or mommy tips. I don't want them to mention that I look tired. I don't want them to ask if I can volunteer for the pancake breakfast, the PTA, or the sport-a-thon.

I know mothers who have their priorities in order. I am not one of them. There are mothers who go to the market with a shopping list and an envelope full of carefully snipped coupons. They make cupcakes with fluffy peaks of whipped frosting and deliver them to the classroom. And they manage to keep their kitchen table free of clutter and get their kids to swimming lessons on time. At least this is how I imagine them when I am questioning my skills as a parent—which is frequently. There are also mothers I absolutely adore and admire for their down-to-earth kindness. And mothers who have saved me from losing my mind by offering to take my kids for the afternoon or evening. While I always considered myself a strong contender in my imaginary International Room Cleaning Competition growing up, as an adult I worry I might be disqualified from entry into the Good Mother pageant.

Rather than clipping coupons or making cupcakes for my daughter's class, what keeps me sane is writing for hours in my lined notebooks or giving myself time to escape into a great book. But while these are the touchstones that keep me grounded, they also lure me away from my responsibilities as an organized and present parent.

Why can't I be a dreamer *and* a good mother? Because I am afraid of what could come of *wanting* things. Isn't that what happened to my mother? She dreamed of who she could be out in the world, forging a brave path, and off she went.

Standing alone in her office bedroom, I stare at the file cabinet. It doesn't feel safe to pull out her letters while others are still awake in the house. What if someone catches me? What if there is something too private and frightening in the letters?

As the night temperature dips and turns the room chilly, I rummage through the upstairs closet for something warm to wear. I find an old wool sweater of Mom's and jackets and hats that I haven't seen her wear in years. I hold up one of my mom's quintessential hippie shirts covered with blue and green paisleys. It has a cigarette hole, and one of the frayed string ties is missing. I haven't seen this shirt since I was eight years old. The summer I finally got to fly to Washington to see where my mom lived.

THEN

all things red

I get to visit my mom in a place called Chimacum. She always lives in towns with interesting names like Sequim and Quilcene, or places with "Port" as part of their name. I am flying by myself this time because my dad already sent my brothers to Chimacum while I was at camp.

The pilot's voice crackles from the tiny holes in the ceiling, announcing that we have made a safe landing in Seattle. I slip on my flip-flops, click off my seat belt, and smooth out the pattern of yellow daisies on my sundress. I give my loose tooth a twist all the way around but I don't want it to fall out just yet. I'm not sure if the tooth fairy comes to Chimacum.

The stewardess in red and blue asks me again who is picking me up.

"My mom might be late," I tell her.

The stewardess looks down at the watch on her wrist. Then I see my mom running down the carpeted walkway and waving both hands in the air. "Little Liddy Bumpkins!" she yells out.

She wears bell-bottom jeans, a strappy black tank top, and red sandals. Brass bells hang down from the bottom of her purse and jingle against her hip. Her wavy hair is longer and darker now. She hugs me big, then steps back to look at me.

"You sure got tan," she says.

She touches the strands of blond hair around my face and asks me if I bleached it. That makes me kind of embarrassed, because I don't know any eight-year-olds who bleach their hair. I look up at her face and suddenly feel like I've got Mexican jumping beans inside me. I want her to like everything about me. I want her to like the daisy dress I picked out.

"How was riding camp?" she asks as we hurry past the crowds.

"Oh, it was the best. I mostly rode a gray horse named Mickey Mouse, but my favorite was a black horse with a white star named Pot Luck."

"Its name was Pot Luck?"

"Yeah, I got to ride Pot Luck after I got bucked off Apache."

"Well, I wish your dad would find some kind of camp for your brothers. They've been going stir-crazy since they got here. They fight like a couple of wild pigs, those two."

I follow the sound of the bells jingling from her hip to keep up with her. There is so much I want to tell her.

"I'm sorry we're rushing, darlin'. It's just that we need to get to the car. If they run the registration on it, we'll be in trouble."

The outside of my mom's car is as dirty and rusty as I've ever seen a car, but the inside smells like coffee with sugar and cream. She reaches across me and fishes through the glove box stuffed with road maps, then pulls out a pack of cigarettes and takes a deep breath.

"I'm living at Ray's this summer, and we've got twin baby goats."

"Who's Ray?" I ask.

"Ray's my boyfriend," she replies with a smile. "He's not used to being around kids, especially your brothers, but I told him how much he'd like you. He's not real talkative. Takes some getting used to, that's all."

"Okay," I reply. But I'm disappointed. I like things better when she doesn't have a boyfriend because then she makes more time for us. I'm wondering if Ray has a beard. Once, she told me that she had "a thing" for beards and liked men with long hair.

"I'm glad your dad let you come, even if it's just for a week. You're going to like Berry Bush Farm. There are ripe blackberries and huckleberries all over the place. We've got the goats—Miss Nanny, Pippin, Opus, and Slope. Then there are the chickens, the flower garden, the cats, and the two geese named George and Martha."

She takes a long drag on her cigarette.

"I've got to warn you about George and Martha though. They can be nasty. They don't like kids or the color red."

"The color red?"

"Well, when Ray wears his red flannels or even a bandanna, the geese come honking and squawking after him. They won't draw blood anymore, 'cause Ray will kick them right across the yard with his steel-toed boot."

I don't like the sound of Ray.

"You ever eaten a goose egg?" my mom asks.

"No, I don't think so."

"Wait until you see one of Martha's cracked open—yolks as big as Florida oranges."

We drive along stretches of quiet highways, and she talks a lot. I'm mostly listening and looking at her face sideways from my seat. I like the way she holds her cigarette against the steering wheel and pauses in the middle of her sentences.

The counselors at camp wanted to know what my mom looked like because of my blond hair and light-colored eyes. Lori Potter said, "I bet your mom is beautiful." And Sandy Deeds asked, "Do you look just like your mom?"

I shrugged because I didn't have a good answer, but now I could tell them more. My eyes are gray, but hers are bright blue with thin crackles in them like the old marbles I have at home. She has a trail of freckles across her nose and I don't have any. We don't really look alike but that's okay with me. I'm just happy to be sitting next to her.

We turn off the main road and bump along a dirt road full of potholes. It's so thick with trees that it feels like we are headed into the wilderness. Branches stick out like arms and screech along the sides of the car. A small house appears, surrounded by an enormous thicket of blackberries, just like my mom said. Animals and chickens are running in all directions as we pull closer. A gray and black goat bounds toward us, leaps onto the hood of the car, and stares at us through the windshield with big amber eyes. I laugh out loud.

"That's my Opus," says my mom. "And here comes Slope, but she won't jump on the car. She's a scaredy-goat."

Then Ray comes out of the house—a big lumberjack of a man with a red beard and a long ponytail to match. He's pale and shirtless. He gives me a nod and a "Hi" from the front porch, then slips his feet into a pair of unlaced work boots.

"Your boys used up the milk again," he says. "I told them Nanny only gives so much."

Behind Ray's big body, I notice the house has no glass in the windowpanes, just sheets of clear plastic stapled up. The paint on the house is the texture of crusty oyster shells.

Jamie and Eden come tearing out of the woods in cutoff shorts. Jamie's furiously waving a stick in the air. Eden doesn't even stop to say hi. Jamie comes to a dead halt. He's completely out of breath, and I can hardly see his eyes beneath his long dirty-blond bangs.

"Hey, Sis, I hope you brought a roll of toilet paper and your shovel, 'cause there's no bathroom in the house."

"Oh sure. Right, Jamie," I say. He always likes to joke around.

"I ain't joking. And I hope you brought a flashlight too, because there are no lights at night."

"Okay, cut it out Jamie, or you'll be sleeping with the chickens tonight," my mom says.

"What for? For telling the truth? Is there a secret toilet somewhere that I don't know about?" He laughs and bolts into the woods after Eden.

My mom smiles at me. "I'm going to explain how things work when we get inside."

I follow her through the screen door, wondering what else I don't know about. The house reeks of sour milk and rotting vegetables. I try not to breathe through my nose. The air is hot and still, trapped by the plastic sheets covering the windows. It is a quick, one-room tour. In the center of the room is a big mattress layered with green army blankets and a torn patchwork quilt. The bedside table is an overturned crate topped with loaded ashtrays, paperback books, and a cigar box overflowing with bangles and glass beads.

"You get to sleep upstairs with the boys. Up there in the rafters." She points. "Just be careful on the ladder. It's very rickety. If you need water, you ask Ray. He can pump it out of the well. And don't listen to your brother. There is a shovel on the porch that always has a roll of paper on the handle, and at night we use kerosene for lighting. You can't expect too many luxuries when the rent is dirt cheap."

"You mean there really is no bathroom here?"

"Well, no proper bathroom, but certainly plenty of trees to pee behind." Then she whispers down to me, "Just don't let Ray catch you going too close to the house. You need to travel out a bit."

Berry Bush Farm is different than I imagined it. I'm wondering if my dad even knows about the no-bathroom situation here. Would he have allowed us to come if he did? I look out through the screen door and see Jamie and Eden setting up plastic army men on grass battlefields. I can hear the *rat-a-tat-tat* of their gunfire, the exploding tanks, and the high-pitched screams of dying soldiers. Eden likes to set the army men on fire and watch them melt.

"You want to go out and play with your brothers?" Mom asks.

"I think I'll go see the goats instead."

I sit down outside with my legs crisscrossed on the brown grass. The twin goats jump high into the air off the hay bales, then run over to Nanny and tug on her teats full of milk. I hold out a handful of dry grass. Opus, the one with the black stripe on his back, comes over, sniffs, then turns up his nose and runs off, kicking his legs in all directions. I laugh because I feel like they are putting on a show for me.

I wander around to the back of the house where I discover a junkyard full of car parts, huge pipes, and old metal containers. I exit through a broken gate and find a million red jewel-like berries spilling over into an old claw-foot bathtub with a rusty bottom. These must be the huckleberries my mom was talking about. I roll a small, red berry between two fingers. It's shiny and smooth like the salmon eggs that my brother fishes with. I pop it into my mouth and can't believe that something can be so sweet and sour at the same time. Here in the hot August sun, I eat handfuls of huckleberries from the old bathtub. Time slows down.

I catch my mom moving through the tall grass on the other side of the yard. She stops between groups of tall yellow and orange flowers. I fill my mouth with one last handful of huckleberries and walk across the yard to her.

"What are you doing, Mom?"

"Taking care of the poppies."

She takes a razor blade and carefully cuts a circle around the bulbous base of the flower. A milky white juice seeps out in little wet dots where she cuts. Then she cuts a second circle around the base, making the flower bulb look like it's adorned in double strands of white pearls.

"That's so neat," I say. "Why are you doing that?"

"They're opium poppies. Don't touch. It makes something special when it dries."

"Could I do that? I like the way white stuff comes out."

She laughs. "You can try it sometime, but not right now. It takes practice."

I continue to watch her do her work. Her fingers full of rings handle the flowers so delicately as her razor cuts into the green skin.

When evening arrives, there is a lot of yelling inside the house. Jamie and Eden are fighting over who has to clean the goat poop on the porch. I get to help light the candles and kerosene lamps in the kitchen. At the table I watch Ray's big hands as he sprinkles dried grass along the crease of a cigarette paper. He rolls it up, licks it closed, and lights it against the candle flame. He and my mom pass it back and forth, holding their breath between turns. It smells just like "grass," the word my dad and his friends use for the stuff they smoke sometimes. I know that grass makes people act differently but I don't get what the big deal is. My dad always sends me away whenever someone lights up a grass cigarette at our house.

I hold my breath because I don't like the smell. My mom will soon slip into a different voice, slow and lazy, like she's from the South. She says she likes to get "high," whatever that means. Maybe this time I will find out what's so great about grass.

I help fill the center of the table with thick, buttery noodles and bowls of fresh chard and other greens from the garden. While we eat, my brothers keep trying to scare me with the idea that we are out in the middle of nowhere, and that there are definitely wolves and bears outside the house at night.

"So just don't be surprised if you wake up in the morning and one of us is missing. Or maybe you'll just find a bloody arm out on the porch," says Jamie.

I ignore them. My tooth is so loose that I can't stop spinning it around in my mouth with my tongue. Ray doesn't say much at the table, other than telling the boys that he is going to throw them outside if they don't pipe down. My mom drinks red wine from a jelly jar and speaks in her slow southern drawl. She kisses Ray in a sloppy way and then sits on his lap and sings: "I went to the animal fair, the birds and the beasts were there…The monkey he got drunk and sat on the elephant's trunk. The elephant sneezed and fell on his knees, and that was the end of the monk, the monk, the monk."

When Ray looks over at me, his eyes are as red as his beard. I turn away because I don't like when people stare at me. And I happen to know that people stare longer when they have been smoking grass. I take a swig from my bottle of orange Fanta and try not to look at my mom or Ray. Eden complains that there's no dessert. Jamie dips his canned sardines into a bowl of ketchup and says he's eating bloody fish. Ray and my mom kiss some more.

I climb up to the rafters, tired and queasy, and lay out my sleeping bag between the two-by-fours. The floor space is divided up into small rectangular plots, so each of us has our own sideboards to prevent us from rolling on top of each other—or off the rafters.

I'm so tired but I can't quiet all the thoughts in my mind. Jamie and Eden are already asleep across from me. I stare at the wooden beams just above my head, watching shadows dance from the candlelight down below. I hear my mom and her boyfriend whispering. When I press my eye to a crack in the floorboards, I can see a thin slice of them. Down below, underneath the torn quilt, he is allowed to touch her skin. He can touch her in a way that I can't. I wonder why she lets him. In this moment,

I hate her. I wish she were more than an occasional mother to us. I imagine her skin, cool and polished like sea glass. I wish that I were Ray, nestled close to her, her warm skin touching me and her arms hugging me until I knew I was safe.

When I wake, it is black all around me. I am full of orange soda and have to pee badly. I recall my brother's words, "Hope you brought your shovel and some toilet paper." But I didn't think about having to pee in the middle of the night. *I can hold it*, I tell myself seven times in a row until I can't any longer. *Shoot, I'm not afraid of bears and wolves.*

I get up as quietly as I can and edge myself down the ladder. I can see through the screen door. *Tiptoe, tiptoe, slow.* I grab onto the spring of the door so it won't creak as I open it, and I slip onto the porch.

I look up at the sky. There is a blanket of brilliant white stars—stars like I have never seen—and the moon is so big that it lights up the whole yard. The scent of ripe berries surrounds me. If only I didn't have to pee so badly.

I step off the porch. Where to go? My mom said to go into the woods, but even with the full moon, it is too dark in the thickness of the trees. I take a left toward the junkyard. Maybe I can find a place near the old bathtub.

And then I freeze. Something is coming at me from out of the shadows. Two beasts side by side. They are ready to attack. I can see it in their red eyes and puffed-up chests. It's George and Martha. The two geese stand in my path with their orange bills raised as high as my shoulders.

"Please, I have to pee," I plead.

I take a step backward. They take a step forward.

I don't even need to look down. I know what are on my feet. I pulled them all the way up to my knees before going to sleep. *Red socks*. Not just any red, but a bright neon red like a clown would wear. The one color the geese hate.

I run back toward the house. George and Martha honk and lunge at me. They continue to chase me—a chicken girl running through the night in red socks. Behind me, their big orange feet pound the earth like elephants'.

I jump onto the porch and turn around. They stop and glare at me. I want to be brave and kick them in the chest like Ray.

"Fine, you stupid geese," I whisper. "I don't have to go anymore anyways."

I slip back into the dark house and stand very still. I think the sound of my heart beating might wake someone but the lumps under the quilt are motionless. A sour milk smell fills my nose again. I tiptoe back up the ladder and crawl to my section of wood. I try crossing my legs together tightly. I try to get in my sleeping bag, but I can't. There are gallons of orange soda inside me. I sneak over to the far corner of the rafters, where the roof touches my backbone, and crouch down as low as I can.

I let it all out. So much inside me. It won't stop. It splatters on the wood, then seeps like hot tea into my red socks. It sounds like there is a faucet on, except this is the house with no running water. I close my eyes until it stops. It is not the smell of orange soda that fills this corner, but the distinct scent of boiled chard water.

Then I hear the worst sound of all—urine spilling through the wood slats and hitting the floor below like hard rain. I jump up and leap into my sleeping bag, tripping across Eden on the way. He stirs.

"What are you doing? What's going on?" he says.

"*Shhh*. Nothing. Go to sleep."

"Yeah, whatever," he says and rolls over.

I push as far into my sleeping bag as I can go. I peel off my wet socks. For all I know, I have peed on Ray's head. What if the paperback books got hit? For a second I feel safe in my sleeping bag, like I'm sealed in a cocoon. But I also have a terrible thought—*I like the idea that I may have peed on Ray's head*. Maybe he'll get so mad that he'll send us away to some motel. A cheap motel with a bathroom that works and no stupid geese. Maybe I will be sent back to California where I am safe with my dad. Maybe my mom will be so disgusted with Ray's peed-on head that she'll leave him.

Then I feel tugged the other way. I think about the sweet and sour huckleberries here in Chimacum, and how the baby goats aren't afraid to jump around and have a ball. Neither are my brothers. But I am. I am afraid of so much, and I don't want my mom to know that I am afraid of anything. Because if I'm afraid of her and Ray and the goats and this strange place, she might not let me come back.

Like the sea turtle at the aquarium, I pull my head out of my sleeping bag. I listen. Everything is quiet and still.

When I wake up in the morning, it feels like a jagged piece of glass is pressing against the inside of my cheek. I reach into my mouth. My baby tooth, clean and white, falls into my palm. I look down over the rafters. My mom is alone, sitting on the mattress with a book and a cigarette. Sheets of newspaper are spread out across the floor like a huge Chinese fan.

She sees me. "I'm sorry about not having a bathroom," she says.

I want to pretend that I don't know what she's talking about or that one of my brothers must have peed in the night. But she points to the floor with her cigarette. "I threw down newspaper, same as you do with a puppy."

I don't want to be the same as a puppy. I want to be her "Little Liddy Bumpkins." As she looks up at me, I get the rules now. I won't drink soda at night. I won't wear red ever again. I'll study her hands and learn to cut the poppies. I'll be tough-skinned like my brothers.

"My tooth came out," I say, excited that I have something to show her. I hold it up in the air like a pearl from an oyster.

She smiles up at me. Her eyes are as blue and open as the sky. "Lemme see, lemme see."

This will be the first tooth of mine that she's ever seen.

I hold on tightly to my baby tooth as I climb barefoot down the ladder toward her.

NOW

faithful

Before boarding the plane to come here to Olympia, Bella told me that her tooth was loose. She always leaves a letter for the tooth fairy underneath her pillow, and her fairy replies with tiny handwritten notes as well as some kind of special treasure—a pearl, a fairy chandelier, an amethyst jewel, a rhinestone button, a crystal teardrop—mostly pieces that sparkle and are the proper size for a fairy to deliver. In my role as the tooth fairy, I revel in finding each treasure. I suppose it comes from what I might have liked as a young girl who believed in good fairies.

I think about calling Bella back to tell her I miss her. It's late. Maybe she's already gone to bed. And I should tell Dominic that I will make time to play cards or watch a movie with him when I get back. But how can I be a parent when I am such a child right now? All of my attention is focused on my mom. I am a small girl waiting for my mother to die.

———

I wait until all the lights are out in the house and then slide open the drawer of my mom's filing cabinet. Her letters are in no particular order and almost none of them are dated, though I'm piecing together a few that clearly date from before she left.

> *I'm absolutely batty in this sinkhole. Dirty diapers staining the floors, strained peas everywhere, and the washer's on the brink. J. is all up in arms because I would like to at least take a week by myself sometime. I can't see where it's such a weird idea. He ought to cut me some slack. I'm inclined to think he's worried about me having a rendezvous with W. and I can't scoff him on that point. But this affinity W. and I have is so totally unrealistic it's ridiculous!*

"W"—I know this refers to Bill, a former "beau" and horse trainer from Texas that she loved and thought about over many years. I met him once when I was thirteen and was struck by how flirtatious my mom was with him. I want to understand how he fits into the timeline of my mom's life. So I read on.

> *J. is out with friends—probably drinking and having fun while I suffer the indignities of attending to numerous tots. We will take our vacation in two weeks. Ah, bliss. Only 6–7 days, but 6–7 days without babies is like 21 with. We'll probably go to Tahoe for a few days and then pan for gold and camp out. I would be so excited if I found a real gold nugget! And it does happen sometimes.*

I don't know if this vacation ever happened or who we would have stayed with for those six to seven days. All I can concentrate on is her hope of finding "a real gold nugget"—so very Mom.

The next note is on composition paper.

I had an English professor once who started out giving me As on all my papers—a thing he didn't do often. Well, he got to know me and my work better, and then gave me Cs. As a way of explanation he called me after class one day in which we had been handed back tests. I had gotten an 86. He asked me if I had seen the movie The Hustler. *I hadn't.*

"Well," he said. "It's about a pool shark, played by Paul Newman, who had so much skill it was hard to believe. He could sink a billiard ball anywhere on the table from any position. But he never won. He was a LOSER, and that's what you are. I'll be damned (he was getting pretty worked up) if it doesn't look like you wanted to keep yourself from getting an A. You sail through so many questions—beautiful, self-respecting, comprehensive answers. The way you did the one on Ophelia was close to brilliant. Then you completely foul up a few as if you thought you were going along too well—as if you weren't going to last. I don't know. We'll see you Thursday."

Oh that man, if he ever realizes what he did to me…or for me?

I never did see him on Thursday. I dropped his course. I wasn't going to mess around with someone who had me pegged. I had good excuses as I was two months' pregnant and

*didn't feel quite up to par when that eight o'clock class rolled
around. But my beloved professor hit me right below the belt.*

Her story devastates me. The thought of my mom, so young
and pregnant, being pegged as a loser and feeling her only choice
was to drop out of her first year of college. Surely this wasn't
what she wanted. My mom was exceptionally bright, and both
she and my aunt received high scores on their IQ tests as young
girls. In hindsight, I think my dad often mentioned this detail
about her IQ because he wanted us to understand that while our
mother didn't always make the smartest decisions, she had the
brains to do so.

While her sister went on to medical school to become a
psychiatrist, my mom's college years ended when she got pregnant with Jamie. But even with an incomplete education, she
was smarter than all of us—at least that was how I felt growing
up. If someone asked me about my mom, one of the first things
I always mentioned was that she was brilliant and had a very
high IQ.

Mindfully, I sift through her letters. I find a letter my mom wrote
to my father but never sent. It appears tear-stained and unfinished.

Dear Jimmy,

*This is going to be a very difficult letter to write in as much
as I really don't know what to say. You have been gone a
month, and that's a very long time to the one left behind.
You left me in a hell of a spot in more ways than one. To me
you were off finding your mind—to everyone else you had*

dumped all your responsibilities and had tooted off to see the
world. I sort of came to the conclusion that since you had
placed yourself as a free and independent person, so would I.
I'd get a job, do whatever I wanted to do—but Good Lord
how could I with Jamie??

It startles me to remember that my dad left briefly too, disappearing for a month when Jamie was nine months old. My
mom had been unfaithful to him, and in a fury he took off and
hitchhiked out to California. As I only know this story from my
father's telling of it, I eagerly keep reading.

Sure I could get a part-time job in the area while Jamie stayed
at home but I don't want that. I don't want Jamie brought up
by my parents or yours. I want him—but not on a "give him
breakfast and kiss him good-night while he stays with some
nanny all day" basis. So what can I do? It's been a case of
deciding what's best for Jamie—to stay with him always and
be miserable for lack of occupation, to get a job and subject
him to no home life whatsoever, or give him up completely so
he'll have a home and I'll spend the rest of my life wanting my
little boy back.
    Look, Jimmy, I failed you—failed you flat and,
therefore, myself. I never made a pleasant home for you
to come into, I've never taken the time to listen and
understand your problems, I've never made an effort to
help you with your work—I've never really, in a nutshell,
tried. And you failed me in some ways, but not nearly as
many. But my selfishness wouldn't let me bend one bit,

though I often wanted to at times. As far as Bill—he's
gone now. Just a memory to put in my memories—believe
me. Over the summer I found that as long as I had other
satisfactions—friends, job—to compensate for troubles on
the home front, I didn't give a damn about William. It
seems as if he's an escape—if I can think I still love him,
I don't have to think that I've made such a mess of things
for nothing. So there! Your payment for desertion. Do you
know that I could have had you arrested?

So she was still thinking about Bill. And from what I know, my dad got to California and picked up a job driving a Buick Riviera for Frank Sinatra and his celebrity pals at the Cal Neva Casino. He'd drive around town with Sammy Davis Jr., Trini Lopez, Gordon MacRae, and Bing Crosby. The tips were fantastic and the parties outlandish—until Frank Sinatra and the Cal Neva were shut down overnight for their associations with Sam Giancana and the mob. That's when my dad headed back to New York, remorseful but committed to making things work out. Eden was born nine months later.

I need you to understand that things have to be different when
you come back and that I very much want to learn how to do
things through love and for love. Oh, there are so many things
we both must understand and they can't all be explained in a
letter. So Jamie and I await your arrival by the 13th. Jamie
has been just fine except for last night when teeth kept the
whole house up all night. These will be 7 and 8, you know!
Even in a month he's gotten to be such a big boy.

This letter gives me such a rare glimpse into my mom and dad as a couple. It also turns my head and heart in different directions. I never knew that my mom called him Jimmy. In her own words, she claims she couldn't stand to have Jamie left with a nanny on an all-day basis. That if she gave him up, she'd spend the rest of her life wanting her little boy back. But could she have ever have imagined that she would someday leave three children behind? What caused her to break away from us and choose the path she did?

NOW

thirst

It is close to two in the morning when I sneak downstairs to the kitchen. I look through the refrigerator and open all the cupboards searching for something to fill me up. I wonder if a beer or a glass of wine would help quiet my addled mind. But as much as that might feel good right now, it feels wrong to drink in this house where alcohol has been my mom's death sentence.

Drinking has never seduced me in quite the same way as it has the rest of my family. I am the only one among my brothers, my mom, and my dad, who doesn't have a DUI on my record. It's one of those facts that would make Jamie laugh and then he'd say something like, "You always were the goody-two-shoes of the family, Sis."

I was twenty when my mom went into rehab and became sober for the first time in my life. She sent me newspaper clippings and articles about the genetic factors and the hereditary curse of alcoholism, and I hoped that this would be the beginning of a closer relationship with her. Alcoholism and addictions killed all four of my grandparents, she explained. She said there was no escaping it.

"You gotta face the facts, Liddy Bumpkins," she told me. "I'm an alcoholic. Your dad's an alcoholic. Your brother is an alcoholic. Your other brother is definitely a drug addict. Our genes are a bloody mess. Even you'd better watch it."

I felt like she was being honest with me, and I wanted to trust her and believe her. I was proud of her recovery. She went back to college, stopped hanging out at the town tavern, and met the man she would later marry. She seemed happy.

I was the opposite. Though I was seeing a therapist at the time, I was all over the place emotionally. I was struggling with my body image and in a hellhole of starving and bingeing. I hated every physical inch of my body. Some days I couldn't get off the floor of my basement apartment. Staring at the dark ceiling beams, I felt a strong thread of connection to my family. I gathered an image of the huge hole in all of us and began to connect the dots, seeing how we each needed to fill it with something: drugs, alcohol, sex, food, whatever.

Maybe I wasn't so different. As I lay there sprawled on the floor, I desperately wanted to let my family know that I was messed up too. That even though I hadn't succumbed to the siren call of alcohol, I was no better than any of them. I was as thin as a snowflake—silent, falling, disappearing. It was my way of coping, of obsessing, of having my own secret addiction. Maybe if they saw I was damaged or really in trouble, there would be something to save.

When I went to see the therapist one afternoon, I told her about a dream that was bothering me. It was one of those dreams in Technicolor that feels entirely too vivid and real. In it, my mom and I are at the beach together having a picnic in the fog with all kinds of delicious cheeses and French baguettes. My mom pulls a bottle of red wine out of the picnic basket and pours a glass for me and a glass for her.

"But Mom," I say, "I thought you didn't drink anymore."

She laughs and says it is "all okay now." I watch her guzzle down the wine.

"You can't do that, Mom. Please." I reach to take the bottle away from her, but my body freezes and I can't lift my arms. I try to tell her to stop, but my voice is gone.

The therapist looked at me as the pause became long and uncomfortable. "You're afraid of losing your mom again, aren't you?"

I turned my head away and looked out the window. It was overcast. Blackbirds dotted the wires between telephone poles. I wondered if the current inside the wires keeps their feet warm.

"It makes sense," my therapist continued. "If she ever goes back to drinking, you might lose her again."

I shook my head. This time would be different.

———

A year later, my mom came down to San Francisco for a visit. We were driving through the rainbow tunnel just beyond the Golden Gate Bridge when she turned to me and said, "Just so you know, I'm having a glass of wine now and then, and it's okay."

I was certain I had misheard her. That as soon as we made it out of the tunnel, she would turn to me and say, "I'm joking, of course." But she didn't. Instead she said there was new research claiming that having "a little bit of wine" was okay—that even some long-time AA drinkers could handle having a glass now and then.

I watched her hand dig deep into her purse for her pack of

cigarettes with a plastic lighter tucked inside the cellophane wrapper. I watched her lips form a seal around the tan filter as she inhaled the lie she was telling herself.

The problem was, there was no such thing as "a little bit of wine" for my mom.

For the rest of the weekend I watched her drink like I had never seen her drink before. She got staggering drunk and then pulled everything out of my kitchen cupboards looking for anything with alcohol. I sat on the tile floor with her as she sobbed and consumed handfuls of Good & Plentys and cried out, "I lost my babies. You have no idea what that was like."

A migraine crawled up my neck and settled in my temples. Everything she said confused me. What did she mean by "lost"? Was there something I didn't know? She seemed angry at me for not understanding her pain—and of course I didn't fully understand. I didn't have children yet. How could I possibly know about the complexities of being a mother or what it would be like to "lose" a baby—or three?

As she continued to rant about the loss of her babies, I knew I should be furious at her for laying all this crap on me. Here was my mother, an inconsolable child, and I had to comfort her because I was afraid she might hurt herself. I wanted to help her out of the addiction she was resurrecting—but I knew I had lost her again. I made her warm tea and got her a blanket when she finally exhausted herself enough to sleep.

"You'll see," she said before drifting off. "I'll make up for it when the grandchildren come."

I had decided that if that time ever came, I would remind her of this promise.

Now as I sit in her kitchen while she drifts away, it's clear she won't be able to keep that promise. For a brief minute, I wonder what it would have been like if she had fully disappeared from my life, never to be seen again. And then a memory skips through me and drops me off in Mrs. Holman's fourth-grade class.

THEN

just off center road

When I walk into my classroom, I notice right away that something is different. Todd Majors is wearing a tie. The girls are all in colorful skirts and dresses. I look down at my square-toed suede boots and want to kick myself. I forgot it was picture day.

My boots are caked with layers of mud from feeding the chickens this morning—but it's not so much the boots as what I threw on in a hurry before running down Center Road to get to school on time. My worn gray T-shirt with "St. Lawrence University" in large, red block letters on the front, my old jean jacket, and my shark-tooth necklace seemed just fine when I left the house. Nobody has to tell me this is not a good choice for picture day. I remember the notice that went home, how it said to wear bright, cheery colors and be "well-groomed." I didn't even make time to tackle the thick knots in my hair this morning.

I sit down at my desk and run my hands along its smooth surface. Even Carmen La Goy is wearing a dress. I stare at her in her blue-and-white-checkered dress with puffy sleeves. She shoots me a dirty look. I can tell she is not happy wearing that dress. Carmen

La Goy, with her silky black hair and a shadow of a mustache above her lip, is the toughest girl in fourth grade. She swears and fights and gets sent to the office frequently. My brother Jamie and his friends call her "La Goy the Boy."

She's usually nice to me though. She tells me I need to toughen up and start swearing, especially since I have brothers. Carmen has two older brothers, and she says she has to fight them all the time. I believe her because she's come to school twice with a fat lip and a purple eye.

Mrs. Holman tells us to line up at the front door because we are going to the auditorium to have our pictures taken.

I approach her desk and say, "I forgot it was picture day."

"I can see that," she replies. I stand at her desk waiting for her to say something more, but she turns abruptly and goes to the front of the line with the "well-groomed" girls, giddy in their flowered dresses and velvet headbands. She huddles around them like a hen. I step back so that I can be at the end of the line. So does Carmen.

Carmen says I'm lucky that I get to wear what I want. "My mom made me wear this stupid spic dress," she says.

I tell her I forgot it was picture day. Then she grabs the sleeve of my jean jacket and says, "Hey, *chica*, we ought to sneak out right now and switch outfits in the girls' bathroom." Her dark, almost black eyes scare me. I don't want to tell her that her dress is a little too frilly even for me.

"I'd love to piss my mom off," she pleads, still hanging on to my sleeve.

I'm grateful when Mrs. Holman escorts us out of the room so I don't have to answer her. On the walk outside to the auditorium, Carmen pulls the barrettes out of her hair. She spits into the oleander bushes and tells me that Mrs. Holman "is pure evil."

In the afternoon, Mrs. Holman calls me and a girl named Tracy Jane up to her desk. I'm certain that she's going to say something about my picture day outfit. But she doesn't. Instead she says, "You know that you two girls have something in common?"

I look at Tracy Jane in her red velvet dress, with her brown curls and shiny white shoes. She seems too large for a fourth grader. Then again, next to Carmen La Goy, I am the shortest in the class. What did I have in common with Tracy Jane?

"You two both live with your fathers," Mrs. Holman says. "You ought to play together sometime."

I shoot a quick look at Tracy, and she eyes me. But then I switch my gaze to the plastic bottle of pink lotion on Mrs. Holman's desk. She is always applying that lotion to her hands—all day long like she's addicted to it. As I watch her pump a wet glob into her palm, I think about how I didn't know anyone else who lived with just their dad. I often picked friends with divorced parents, but none of them ever lived with their dad. Maybe Mrs. Holman isn't so bad. Maybe she is trying to keep me from hanging out with girls like Carmen La Goy.

Tracy and I don't talk to each other like Mrs. Holman suggested. But I catch her looking at me from across the room. Or maybe she is the one who notices me staring at her. It's not until Mrs. Holman pairs us up for tetherball that we start talking. Tracy hits the ball hard at me and asks me if I like horses.

"Like horses? I love horses," I say, hitting the ball back.

"I've got a whole shelf full of Breyer statue horses in my room," she tells me.

"Do you have Man O'War?" I ask.

"No, but I want him. My newest one is Midnight Sun."

I know exactly which one she's talking about. Midnight Sun is a black Tennessee Walker with red and white ribbons streaming from his mane.

She says she's not allowed to go over to other people's houses, but that maybe I could come over to her house after school sometime to see her horse collection. "Sure," I tell her, "My dad doesn't mind."

We don't talk much more after that, but I make a plan to go to her house two days later.

———

On Thursday after school, we walk together down Center Road toward Tracy's house. Everything in our town seems to be just off Center Road. I'm thinking of all the questions I have for Tracy. As it turns out, she lives on the same court as Carmen La Goy, who races past us on her silver boy's bike without saying a word. We pass Storybook Court and Stanford Court. I'd like to live on one of those cul-de-sacs where all the kids play together in the evenings—where they have streetlights between the houses. The long driveway that leads to our yellow house turns into a pitch-black alley once the sun sets. It's the reason no one ever comes trick-or-treating to our house on Halloween.

As I walk with Tracy, I step over the lines on the sidewalk. *Step on a crack, break your mother's back,* I say to myself.

I want to ask Tracy about her mom. I'm wondering if maybe her mom lives in another state too. I've already imagined how much we have in common, how maybe our moms even know each other.

"My mom lives in Washington. The state," I tell her.

"Oh," she says. "My house is that brown and white one at the end of the court."

We pass Carmen La Goy's silver bike thrown down on the sidewalk outside her house. A lot of yelling in Spanish is coming from inside the house.

"There's always screaming at Carmen's house," Tracy tells me. "I'm not supposed to walk on this side of the street any-more." Tracy suddenly veers across the road and I am a step behind her.

"So where does your mom live?" I ask.

"My mom is dead," she says.

"Oh," I say. I keep my eyes down on her shiny white shoes.

"Yeah. You want to know how she died?" She sounds almost perky all of a sudden.

"Alright," I say, stepping carefully over the cracks.

"She hung herself on my fifth birthday. Right in our garage. With a rope."

The sidewalk turns wavy, back and forth like the lines are trying to trick me. I want to turn around and run. But it's too late. Tracy opens the front door to her brown and white house and calls out to her dad.

Her dad is old, way older than my dad. He has silver hair and deep creases across his forehead. He's holding a curvy pipe in one hand, while the other hand is pushing a wooden spoon deep into a cooking pot on the stove. The smell of meat and musty pipe smoke fills the kitchen.

"This is Melissa, Daddy," Tracy says.

He says hello with the pipe still pushed in his mouth and keeps stirring the pot. Tracy gets on her toes to look into the pot.

"What's in there?" she asks.

"Stew," he says. Then the room is quiet, except for a fan whirring above the stove. I want to look into the pot and see what the stew looks like because I wonder if Tracy's dad put dumplings in his stew. Stew isn't stew without thick, gummy dumplings floating on the surface.

Tracy motions for me to follow her down the hallway. Just like she said, she has a shelf full of statue horses—more than I have ever seen. There are colorful posters of horses thumb-tacked on her walls. She has a bedspread with pink horseshoes on it.

I'd like to keep my mind on all the horses, but all I can think about is what Tracy said about her mom. Why would her mom hang herself? On Tracy's birthday? Maybe Tracy Jane is one of those kids like Eden who lies and makes up stories sometimes.

We talk about horses for a little while. She has a palomino with a gold bridle that I love more than any of the others in her collection. It's the one I've always wanted. But I'm not a very good guest at her house. I keep thinking about her mom. I have a terrible picture in my mind of what she looked like when she was hanging. My stomach is twisted up like the towels when they come out of the washing machine.

Tracy perks up again. "You want to see the garage where my mom hung herself?"

"No, that's okay."

She looks very disappointed with me and grabs the palomino horse out of my hand. "You have to, Melissa, because I say so and besides I've got more horse things in the garage."

She stands up, and I feel so small and out of place sitting on the floor of her bedroom. I look at the palomino horse dangling from her hand, and I know that I am never going to have one like that.

She tells me that we have to sneak past her dad in the kitchen. But as soon as Tracy starts to open the side door to the garage, her dad comes toward us with the long spoon still dripping with stew. "How many times?" he yells. "Out. Now!"

I know now that what Tracy said about her mom is true. I see it in her skittish brown eyes and I hear it in the rattle of her dad's voice. It is horrible and scary, and I don't want to be here.

"I have to go home now," I say.

Tracy gallops like a horse down the hallway and slams her bedroom door shut. Her dad goes back to stirring the pot on the stove. There are no dumplings in that stew; I don't even have to look.

I see myself to the front door. I want to run down the street, but I measure my steps, careful not to step on the cracks. I pass Carmen's bike, still out on the sidewalk. I think about her riding that bike in the blue-and-white-checkered dress on picture day, and how things are not always as they seem. I think about the pink lotion that Mrs. Holman covers her hands with every day. I think about Tracy's mom, and I wonder what she was wearing that day in the garage.

As I cross onto Center Road, there is no road I would rather be on right now. I don't want to live on Storybook Court or one of those cul-de-sacs, or on the same street as Tracy Jane and Carmen La Goy. For now, the big yellow house off Center Road is just fine with me.

NOW

naked

I've lost my sense of time here at my mom's blue farmhouse. I wait, I eat, I hide, I wait. I sit next to her, I read. I drift off to sleep with her letters hidden beneath the bed. I wake, I read. There is no logical sequence to my mom's letters and dabbles. Why does she refuse to date anything? I need order right now. As I read through more, I'm piecing together a patchwork quilt of papers and trying to stitch them all together. There must be some secret sewn into the edges here or a dark thread that will lead me closer to understanding her.

I find a card she never sent that is addressed to me, or Lou-lah, as she liked to call me sometimes.

My Dear Lou-lah,

As yet, things are uncertain about the future. I long to be with you and will do all that I can to make that happen. In the meantime this card, although not too well designed, expresses a bit of my feelings. I DO want the rainbow to touch your shoulder always. May you be surrounded by all the colors to light your way. I love you, sweets—XOXO, keep it in mind.

The first time I saw the series of Xs and Os at the bottom of one of the letters she sent to me growing up, I didn't know what they meant. Was it some kind of code that I needed to figure out? Our live-in at the time explained that the Xs were kisses and the Os were hugs. I liked the symbols she was sending.

Back at home, I have a nine-by-twelve envelope that contains each of the letters my mother sent me when I was growing up. Though she rarely saw us, she sometimes sent us cards and letters. The postmarked envelopes are from different towns, the stationery from different stores. Some letters were written on light-blue airmail paper, others on small, lined sheets with perforated edges, and a few on white butcher paper from the time my mom lived with the meat cutter. Many of her letters are written with a black cartridge pen on opaque paper— "onion-skin parchment," she liked to call it. A few are typed—those are from the later years.

I prefer the letters written in her beautiful black ink. As a child, I wanted nothing more than to have handwriting like hers—something between cursive and calligraphy and print. So uniquely her, lovely and free-spirited.

I remember getting her letters and trying to copy her handwriting, but I could never match it. It was like she had the exclusive rights to the style. But I changed the way I scripted my letters anyway, in hopes that someday my hands would move across the page in the same way hers did.

Because I usually couldn't see her in person, I fell in love with her words, the ink, the feel of onion-skin paper, and the way she phrased things in clever ways. She was smart with words—*New York Times* crossword puzzle smart. She played with

made-up words and double meanings. There were often words—
even whole sentences—that I couldn't quite understand, but I
didn't mind because the words were meant for me.

Now I'm finding these passages from a long-lost story. Her
letters never sent—and addressed to no one in particular.

Hallo!

*I was a bit startled when I woke last night with regular pains,
but they abated by morning. I saw the doctor last week, and
though he is a wonderful fellow, I'm furious at him. I was
counting on having a nice little baby in August, but he says
that he counts on an "oversize baby in September." Happy
days. I'll fool him—though my weight is really out of control.
I try to diet, but my appetite knows no bounds. Actually, I
am keeping down somewhat, but every ounce shows in an
"unpregnant fashion." Our family physician has promised to
rid me of all the ill effects of my frequent childbearing—broken
capillaries and what not—and is awaiting J.'s word on making
certain I don't get pregnant again. I don't voice my opinions
to J., but I certainly am tired, tired, tired of bulging bellies and
messy diapers and no-no's. I love my babies, but I am sort of
swamped. My "light" is the realization that it is possible that
I can have my family, be through with the constant pressure
babies give, and still be 25 or 26.*

She's surely referring to my arrival here since I came into
world on August 21. Perhaps from the womb, I heard her wishes
for me to come early. There's a nagging question though. She's

clearly overwhelmed but not to the breaking point. Was I the one that pushed her past the point of no return and caused her to come undone?

Impulsively, I shut the door of the bedroom and strip off all of my clothes. I stand naked in front of a full-length mirror, daring to see my body exposed. I hold onto such shame and hate when I look at my body. I don't know when this first began. My long and lean torso comes from my mother. My petite stature, from my grandmother Rita who had narrow hips and birdlike bones.

The structure of my cheekbones and the arches of my eyebrows come from my other grandmother, the glamorous Joan Igou, who danced on Broadway and died too young. And from my father comes the distinct slope of my Irish nose. Several times, my mother suggested I have it "bobbed" as soon as I turned eighteen because it was going to grow too long on my small face.

I used to think that my eyes were an interesting shade of blue like that of a blue-winged teal, but they have turned gritty and gray. My golden hair, now wavy and unruly. And then there is the birthmark on the small of my back that is the shape of a tiny country. France, says my husband. And these breasts have never been big enough, except for the years I nursed my son and daughter. (Then, they were full and fantastic!)

In light of my mom's bodily angst, I want to accept this naked armor of mine—its vitality, endurance, and strength. But here and now, all that's apparent is that my body, like my mother's, will someday fail me. Where is the girl with long, blond hair and bright eyes, the one who could gallop a horse full speed and ride unaccompanied through the woods at night? Where is the girl who once ran naked and unashamed into the ocean?

NOW

tethered

I wake up groggy and unclear about what day it is and if I'm still in Olympia. I've had a horrible dream. In the dream, I see my mom up close—but physically we are a thousand miles apart. She is standing on a hardwood floor wearing yellow. That should have been a clue that I was dreaming. She hates yellow.

I call out to her, "Mom!"

She nods and acknowledges me from a distance—a thousand miles away, yet somehow in view. She watches me as I hunch over and clutch my stomach. I am bleeding. There are cramps deep inside me and I feel something slipping out of me. Like afterbirth or bits of placenta—like the wobbly pieces of thick blood that came out of me in the days after my children were born.

But when I see her face, I see that she is in pain too. She also is doubled over. I try to understand what is happening between us. Then I realize what is coming out of me: it is her liver, in pieces, sliding out of me. I squeeze my legs together to keep it all in. But the pieces are thick, slippery, and filled with veins and blood.

My mom's diseased liver is coming out of me. I am birthing it, delivering it. I shove my hands between my legs to push it back. But the contractions are too strong. We are a thousand miles apart and there is nothing we can do to stop it.

Shaking myself fully awake, I hear voices downstairs, coming from my mom's room. I put on the same sweater and jeans I've worn for the past three days and go down to hear the hospice nurse speaking loudly. When I turn the corner, I see my mom propped up with pillows.

She looks at me and says, "Hi, darlin'."

Am I still in the dream? She has color in her face. Her eyes look blue. She recognizes me for the first time since I arrived. She seems to have come back from the edge of death.

"Your mom is just amazing," the hospice nurse says to me. "She looks great today."

My heart is nervous and kicking. "Hi, Mom."

"Mikel, you've rallied!" my aunt says.

Rallied, I think to myself. *What does that mean?* This is the nurse who said Mom wasn't going to make it to the new year, and now my mom is sitting up in bed looking like she's going to ask for a cigarette and a plate of prime rib.

I watch the nurse take my mom's vital signs and rub her feet. My emotions are racing around the room, uncertain of where to rest. *She recognizes me.* This is closer to how I remember her looking the last time I was here in Olympia.

I want to say that I'm relieved and filled with joy that my mom has rallied, but I am confused. My best friend Alison's words race back to me: *"You only get one chance to hold your mother's dying hand."* When she said this to me after I called to tell her the news about my mom on Christmas Day, I knew I had to come. Alison's mom died when we were growing up, and

Alison was there in the hospital holding her mom's hand when she stopped breathing. I want this last moment. Yet I promised my daughter that I'd be back by New Year's Eve to welcome in the new year as well, and that date is creeping closer and closer. How long does a rally last? I can't stay here indefinitely.

I transfer my gaze to the collection of colored bottles on the windowsill beside my mother's bed, ashamed to make eye contact with anyone in the room. Afraid that I am transparent. I don't want her to know that I have her letters and was reading them. There must be some reason for her to have woken up like this. Does it mean that I will have the opportunity to connect with her before she dies? Could it be that she woke up to tell me the things she has always wanted to say? Is there some treasure she will put in my hands?

My mom's little dog Sparky—a Toto look-alike—parks herself near my feet. I reach down and rub her black and gray fur. I recall how my mom said she wanted to give Sparky away a few years back.

"She's too needy," my mom told me.

"I should leave Sparky here at your house," she said to Bella on a brief visit to Los Angeles.

Bella stared at her grandmother in disbelief. "Why would you do that?"

"Oh, she might like living here with you."

"But you're her mom. She would miss you too much."

Sensible Bella, calling it right. But I had to wonder if there was a pattern emerging. Every time that something seemed to become a responsibility in my mom's life, she dumped it or ran away. Was that perhaps why she left us as well?

The hospice nurse talks fast and louder than anyone else in the room, as if she is the announcer on a game show. I am irritated by her cheerfulness. She parcels out handfuls of colorful pills into their tiny compartments. Why did I believe her proclamation about how much time my mom had left?

I sit near my mom, lean over, and give her a cautious hug. She's feels light in my arms—a tumbleweed I have been chasing for years. She asks me how the "kidlets" are. Maybe I *should* have brought them so she could see them one last time.

My mom says she'd like to go outside to feed some apples to the ponies. "Sure!" replies the hospice nurse. The thought of walking next to her through the crisp winter air lifts my spirits.

But after she sits up awhile longer and doesn't succeed in swallowing anything other than her medication, it's clear that the journey across the yard to the ponies will be too strenuous.

As soon as the nurse helps guide my mom into the bathroom and closes the door, I run upstairs to put the letters back in the file cabinet so no one can tell I've been snooping around. I wish I knew what to say to my mom now that she is awake. I am confronted by the familiar distance between us and the way I suddenly become smaller in her presence. Her personality has always been bigger, more theatrical and colorful than mine.

Unable to bring myself to go back downstairs just yet, I call home but there is no answer. I'll wait until I hear the hospice nurse shut the door and drive away from here. I am ashamed that I am not downstairs right now, spending every moment with my mom. Instead, I'm alone again, looking for something to ease the reality of what is happening. I reach back into the folder of letters never sent.

I must sit—even though I can't find a proper pen—pencil will have to suffice while I wait for my pie's fate in the oven. If I don't watch it, Eden will come toddling off the potty and gobble up my Cuba Libre before I can say Phhftt. And then he'll be sauced—in as much as a Cuba Libre is a hoity-toity for rum and Coke—same type pseudo as Shirley Temple— and will be more of a pill than ever. He is off his bottle but back on his tranquilizers. Poor little creature is either deadpan or flooded with emotion. He got so excited in the kiddie pool this afternoon that he just lay flat down on his back and nearly drowned. So funny—he was scared to death of the thing at first but now he's like a bloomin' porpoise. He charges like a bull elephant and flings himself headfirst into a foot of water. This can hurt but he couldn't care less—even about scraping his shins on the side which he inevitably does.

Eden was put on tranquilizers as a toddler? This is utterly distressing, especially considering how Eden has struggled with substance abuse for much of his life since then. Did he get hooked as a little boy? While I understand the desire to calm an overactive child at whatever cost, I cannot imagine what my mom was thinking. Wasn't she the one that might have benefited from something to ease her own anxiety and depression?

And:

Life is life. Melissa is an absolute lovie supreme. She's a true-blue, dyed-in-the-wool butterball with rolls and rolls of fat all over. It's true what they say about little girls being able to work magic spells.

I didn't have a magic spell, Mom. I couldn't make you stay then or now.

Jamie is himself—smart-aleck mouth to boot. His favorite expressions: "Okay, I don't think I like you anymore!" or "I'm going to tell my dad on you." He leads his "pack" up and down the street with great authority, even though he's at least a year younger than the rest, and he is the love of the neighborhood. Honestly, I hardly see him all day—even when most of his friends are in school—it's the mothers inviting him in for a visit. Bet he doesn't sass them!! He loves Melissa and had one of the most upsetting moments in his life when one of the older kids told him that she was not his baby sister.

Eden—well, I'm a bit worried about Eden. His little psyche is suffering dreadfully. He's prone to fits that make one think he has a completely uncontrollable temper—until you see how often he has them. So sad. Even when he's playing very happily by himself with his toys, he'll suddenly fly into a rage and throw himself from wall to wall and upon the floor. I'm going to the doctor to talk about it as I can't quite believe it all has to do with being somewhat spoiled.

Spoiled? I don't think Jamie, Eden, or I would ever use this word in thinking about our upbringing. And, yes—poor Eden. What was going on with him? Did the tranquilizers exacerbate the anger he frequently showed? He and Jamie often got into fistfights with other kids at school because they couldn't control their rage. In my recollection, Eden didn't win fights; he just fought to survive. Jamie was the cool cat on the school yard, Eden the gangly kid who got picked on. I always wanted to root for Eden, the underdog, but sometimes he took his anger out on me.

THEN

warmth

When Jack Frost arrives in early spring Jamie, Eden, and I find our way to the center of house where our old floor heater ticks, purrs, and blows hot, dusty air into the hallway. We line up, three across, and stand over the grate with our legs apart until it gets too hot and the metal edge starts to burn the bottoms of our feet. Our dad says the fifty-year-old heater is a fire hazard but we don't care. It's the warmest spot in the house and the place we gather on cold mornings before school.

"Scoot over," says Eden, eleven, bare chested, and shivering in his Fruit-of-the-Loom underwear.

He says I'm hogging the heater because all the good air is blowing into my nightgown. Jamie bumps Eden out to the edge and tells him to stop acting like a girl.

"Watch this one," says Jamie as he leans over and spits into the rectangular metal grate.

"You missed," says Eden, who follows and hits the center.

They like to watch their spit sizzle and fry on the metal burners. They are not supposed to do it—Dad will be furious.

"I'm telling," I say. But they know I won't because they remind me that I tried it once too. I did try it. It makes a strange smell like hair when it gets singed over a stove burner.

This morning, I hold my spot. Our dad comes down the stairs buttoning up a Pendleton shirt. He says he's making a run to 7-Eleven for Frosted Flakes and milk. He turns back, commanding Eden's attention.

"I want you off this heater and dressed for school by the time I get back. You understand?"

Eden shifts his feet back and forth along the metal grate. "Yeah, yeah," he says back.

"Don't 'yeah-yeah' me," says my dad, already angry.

The two of them are mad almost every morning these days because Eden won't get out of bed without a fight. When he finally does get out of his bed, he stands hunched over in his underwear on the heater—and that's a whole other fight.

As soon as my dad walks out the door, I tell Eden, "You're supposed to get dressed."

"Shut up," he says back to me.

I don't want them to have a fight this morning. I know how long it takes to get to 7-Eleven and back. It's pretty much a straight shot down Center Road.

"I'm out of here," says Jamie, already dressed and pulling his black beanie on. He heads out the front door with a jar of mustard in his hand and half a dry salami sticking out of his back pocket. I get dressed quickly in my room, hoping that Eden is off the heater when I open my door. But he's there.

I make another attempt. "You know, Dad is going to be back any second."

He says nothing. I step back onto the heater.

"Okay, make some room at least," I say.

I don't see his fist coming at me.

He slugs me square in the face.

Beneath me, I hear the sizzle sound. But it's different from the spit frying. It's blood hissing against the hot metal.

I want to cry, but I look him straight in his blue eyes instead. I look for something in him, something that will make me believe that he didn't mean it, that he's sorry. But I don't see anything except my brother who is always mad these days, my brother who pulls apart insects and lights things on fire. He turns and walks away from the warmth of the heater.

I let the blood drip from my nose. I watch it splatter into black spots on the metal. It dries fast. *Blood*, I think…different from spit, more sharp smelling.

NOW

inside out

I was wary around Eden after the incident on the heater. But there was also a side of my middle brother that was kind and wise and patient. I remember catching him in my room after he had pried the musical component out of my dancing ballerina music box.

"It's not right to take apart things that aren't yours!" I yelled.

And he said, "You gotta see how this works inside."

Then he showed me that I could still play the music and that now I could *see* how it was made by tiny metal spikes all going around in a certain order. As the spool of spikes hit the small bobby-pin fingers, I could feel the movement and cadence of the "Hi-Lili, Hi-Lo" song right through the palm of my hand. I kept running my fingers along the sharp moving parts that could make up a whole song. It was simple magic. Copper and steel wires, small metal screws, a spool of spikes, sound and order.

We sat together on the floor, not needing to say anything to each other. I understood that he was showing me something—that when things are hidden inside, you can't possibly know how they work. If you take something apart and really look at it, hold it, and touch it, you can understand it much better.

I search deep in the folder of letters for any other clues about Eden. Instead, I find this one scrawled on torn pink stationery:

Gee, golly damn, there is so much to learn—to think over and decide about. I feel so righteous every time I come to a decision but I never have enough of a basis. Personally, it has been a rather low period. I hope that it doesn't get much lower, or that any reactions I might have don't cause havoc with anyone. How I hate my bitchiness when any little thing goes wrong. It used to be just when I was tired or particularly worked up. But now it is far too frequent and J. and the children suffer, and I do mean suffer—every day. But ever realizing this, I cannot help myself. I am pulling further and further away— their suffering affects me less and less. But is that not natural when I suffer more and more? I don't suffer from anything but myself. They try so hard to be good to me, and I have to be sick to keep pushing such goodness away. If only I could talk to someone. Medea must have suffered too.

I look out the window, watching the winter rain trickle down the glass. Medea killed her children. In the Greek tragedy by Euripides, she was a highly intelligent woman who allowed passion to rule her actions. These words of my mother's so clearly spell out depression and desperation. For the first time ever, I think, *Maybe it was a good thing she walked out and that we had all those live-ins.* And then I remember my visit to Valley View Farm.

THEN

the last litter

Valley View is a nice place to visit my mom—a lot better than the last place, which had no electricity or toilet. I get to stay for almost a week, and I even get to be here for my tenth birthday. There's a bed with a blue quilt, a shelf piled high with boxes of puzzles, and the scent of my mom's L'Air du Temps perfume drifting down the hallway. She lives on this dairy farm with one hundred eighty cows and her new boyfriend, Roger Short.

One of the first things she mentioned about Roger is that he's color-blind. She says he can't see how horrible the wall-to-wall chartreuse carpet looks in his house—in fact he can't see the color green at all. I think that's a shame, because there are green fields like patchwork for miles around his farm. But then again, I suppose that being color-blind is just fine for Roger since he only raises black and white cows.

My mom pours the warmed milk from the stove into oversize plastic bottles and then pops on the giant caramel-colored nipples.

"Do you want to feed one of the little ones down in the calf barn?" she asks.

I cannot contain my smile. My Keds are on in three seconds.

I follow her down the grassy path, holding the warm milk bottles against my chest, and try to copy the sway of her hips. She explains how the calf barn is the holding place for the young Holstein calves who are being weaned from their mothers' milk.

"Roger likes to wean them young," she tells me, "so that the mother cows can get back to their job of being milk cows."

When they see us with the milk bottles, the calves cry and bleat like goats. A black and white calf shoves his head through the wooden slats of the stall and stares up at me with his big polished eyes. I place the rubbery nipple close to his mouth. He grabs and tugs fiercely at the bottle.

"Hold on tight," my mom says. "That guy is a tough little sucker."

My calf slurps as he drinks, then yanks at the nipple like he's mad at it. Milk splatters across his soft black face. When he's done with the milk, he wants to keep chewing and sucking on the rubber tip, but my mom says that will put too much air in his stomach.

"Just stick two fingers in his mouth," she tells me from across the aisle.

"What?" I say.

She walks over to my calf and sticks her middle and pointer finger right into his mouth. He latches on and starts making sucking sounds.

"There are no teeth in there, just gums," she says.

I hesitate, not certain about this. She grabs my hand and pulls it toward the calf's mouth. He latches onto my two fingers with such force that I am startled. His mouth is strong and smooth inside. I feel his tongue, like fine sandpaper scrubbing my fingers. I start to laugh. My mom laughs too. I don't want this to stop. I take my other hand and rub the calf's face, admiring the swirls of thick, black velvet and the lopsided white diamond on his forehead.

My mom says she's got a few chores to do back at the house, and I ask if I can stay here in the calf barn for a while. "I like it here," I tell her.

"I'm glad," she says. She smiles at me, pushes an unlit cigarette into her mouth, and gathers up the empty milk bottles.

My fingers have become a little sore from staying in the calf's mouth so I pull them out. The calf seems okay because after a minute he buckles down on his wobbly legs and flops onto the straw floor. I decide to do a little exploring around the barn. There are dusty bird's nests tucked all around the rafters and small starlings that swoop down to gather bits of straw from the ground. I find a place to sit in the feed room where there are burlap sacks filled with cracked corn and molasses-covered oats. I push my hands deep into the open sacks and pull the molasses oats close to my nose. They smell good enough to eat.

I take a walk to the far end of the barn aisle where the calf stalls are empty. There are two tall, white buckets with lids on them, the plastic kind that painters use. They look out of place to me for some reason, like maybe they were set down there and forgotten. I pry the lid off the bucket closest to me. There is no particular smell.

I am not sure if what I am seeing is right or true. Kittens. Piled up to the brim. Clean white fur. Brown, black, tan, orange. Small paws with fleshy pads as soft as apricot skin. Wiry tails. Tiny pink noses. Whiskers, as fine as fishing line, almost transparent.

It is not a dream. I push the lid back on. I think that there must be more than a dozen piled up in there. I pry open the other bucket, only because I want it to be something different. But it's not. One all black, one striped orange, one smoky gray, more colors underneath. Soft triangle ears, thin as potato chips. I want to stop staring but I can't. A small calico kitten lies across the top of the heap. Its eyes are closed, but the shallow part of its belly moves—barely, up and down like it's in a deep sleep. I want to touch it, but I am afraid. I don't know what to do so I put the lid back on.

I walk back up the hill toward the farmhouse, my heart thumping underneath my yellow T-shirt, the tall wet grass soaking the bottoms of my jeans. When I open the screen door, I see my mom at the table with her *New York Times* crossword puzzle, her coffee, and a cigarette. She's smart with words. I'm not. I have a throat full of gravel that keeps me from saying what I want to say. But this time my question forces its way out.

"Why are all those kittens in the white buckets?" I ask.

She keeps looking down at her crossword puzzle as if she's just about to figure something out. Her sandy bangs hang like a frayed curtain across her forehead. Twenty to thirty seconds pass and I begin to think she's not going to answer my question.

"Oh, that," she says with a frown. "You *weren't* supposed to see that. Roger was supposed to dump them."

I wait for her to say something more.

"I'm sorry you had to see that, darlin'. It's the way of the farm here."

That's it? That's all she's going to say? She smashes the clump of soft ashes down with the filter of her cigarette. There is sparkly pink polish on her fingernails. I hate it when she's so matter-of-fact.

"There were just too many kittens."

"What do you mean, too many?" I ask.

"Those were feral kittens, wild and inbred—just the ugly ones. Believe me. I can tell the inbred ones right away, their eyes are wide-set and slightly askew. Their heads are oversized."

"But how did they die?"

My mom gets up from the table with her ceramic coffee cup and goes into the kitchen. I can tell she doesn't want to listen to my questions.

"Chloroform is what Roger said to use." She measures a heaping spoonful of sugar into her cup. "But power-steering fluid works just as well. It's very quick. They don't suffer."

I feel my throat tighten up like a fist. My legs are as wobbly and uncertain as the calves down in the barn.

"Mom, I saw one breathing on the top. A calico one. Not an ugly one, but a long-haired calico."

"There were no calicos," she says, slamming the garbage-can lid down. "And you *did not* see any kittens breathing."

"I did, Mom. I definitely saw that one on top."

"None of those kittens were breathing, you understand?"

I am suddenly afraid of her. She knows how much I love kittens, and I know there was a calico. I try to stop the image of her hands pushing those kittens into the white buckets.

She heads out the screen door, says she has to grab a few fresh eggs and she'll be right back.

I watch her outside the window, walking through the tall grass. I recall what I once overheard her say—that she thought about drugging my brothers and me when we were small because she didn't want us to suffer. She had an emergency plan in case there was an awful natural disaster. She would give us all sleeping pills. We wouldn't suffer. But I am almost ten now and I am too big to trick like that.

I wait at the window for her to come back, willing myself not to think about the kittens. I want to feed the calves with her again. I want to swirl the sugar and cream into her coffee and breathe in her L'Air du Temps perfume. I want her to like me. I'm tired of not knowing the next time I'll see her. I scratch my fingernail along the thin, white paint that covers the windowsill, reminding myself that it's better to keep my secrets inside.

I am not supposed to remember the day she drove away in her baby-blue Dodge Dart. Everyone tells me that I was too young to remember. But I remember everything. "Too many," she said. I know this phrase well. I heard her screaming it late one night at my dad before she left us. Three kids were too many. I was the third.

I shove my hands into my jean pockets and push those secrets in as far as they will go. I make room for the kittens, because they are a new secret.

NOW

ashes, ashes

"Melissa, are you coming back down?" my aunt calls from the bottom of the stairs.

I close the file cabinet.

My mom sits slumped on the toilet. She asks me to bring her a magazine and a cigarette. "Do you really need a cigarette, Mom?" I ask.

"I do," she says.

"Okay…"

I don't know how her body can even absorb a cigarette at this point. She can hardly straighten her spine. I light a cigarette and hold it up to her lips. As weak as she is, she clamps down on the filter and manages to inhale. Her eyes roll back and I detect a flash of pleasure—but then it is gone, like a bird just flew through the room and out the window. Why am I feeding my mom a cigarette when she cannot eat solid food anymore?

"How about a magazine?" she asks.

I ask her what kind of magazine she wants, and she says it doesn't matter. I know that she stopped reading months ago. The buildup of ammonia in her brain keeps her mind in a fog.

She can't track thoughts in order. She cannot follow words on a page.

Her mother died at forty-six. "Drank herself to death" was how I always heard it from my mom. I never got to meet my grandmother but I learned she was a Ford fashion model, a dark, brooding Joan Crawford type with translucent skin and intense eyes. She danced on Broadway with Buddy Ebsen and had a studio contract to go on with her film career. Somewhere early on, she lost her way.

I have her journals, her modeling portfolio, and the old promotional posters from her debut movie, *Titans of the Deep*. My mom gave me them years ago when she wanted to rid her life of memories that were too sad for her all of a sudden. In the red leather journal inside my desk drawer back at home, my grandmother writes: "If I ever marry and settle down to a mediocre family life, and accept the plebeian life, I will regret it every day of my existence."

She settled and had three children, my mom being the youngest. Her only son was killed in an avalanche as a teenager, along with six other boys, during a summer wilderness camp. It was national news in July 1955. An ironic detail was that the boys had traveled in a used hearse to their destination in the Canadian Rockies. Within five years of the accident, my grandmother was dead from the same kind of alcoholic liver cirrhosis that her daughter is now dying from.

I grab a *National Geographic* off the bathroom sink and set it on my mom's lap. She opens it and rubs her fingers along the corners of the glossy pages. I sit on the edge of the tub in front of her, ready to catch her if she loses her balance.

She pretends to be reading something on the page but her mind is somewhere else. I feel like she's trying to show me that she's okay, that she can still do the things she's always done. She is pretending to read and I am pretending that this does not break my heart. She's trying so hard to stay in this world now.

"Am I ever going to get my mind back?" she asks as she holds on to the edge of the page. I cannot answer this question for her. My throat is full of dry leaves. It hurts to swallow. All I can do now is keep her cigarette burning so that she can at least have the familiar scent of smoke as she breathes. And I know this is all wrong. She watched her father die of lung cancer after his years of smoking two packs of Pall Malls a day.

What if he could see his daughter right now? And what would he say to me, here, holding on to her last cigarette? I want to shout out to him that she has done this damage to herself. She didn't want to give up drinking, and now it is going to kill her. She will die the same way her gorgeous mother did at forty-six. A body full of bad fruit and a beautiful mind losing all reason and empathy. Why must history be repeated? And what can I do to change the course of things to come?

When my mom drifts off to sleep again, I retreat upstairs and open her file of letters never sent. The brittle newspaper clipping is tucked into the manila folder. It is stapled to several sheets of lined paper with my mom's handwriting. The scent of aged paper creeps into my sinuses as I unfold the creases. The brief article reads:

ASHES OF CLIMBER REST ON MOUNTAIN

Alberta, Canada—July 28, 1955

The ashes that were the last mortal remains of a 15-year-old Philadelphia schoolboy were scattered Tuesday over the towering slopes of Mount Temple in Banff National Park, writing the finish to a tragedy that stirred a continent. Young David Chapin was one of seven teenaged climbers who perished July 11 when an avalanche thundered down on them at the 9,500-foot level of the treacherous peak. Only four of the party of 11 that started the climb survived. The boy's heartbroken parents felt that the slope on which he had spent his last moments would be the fitting resting place for his body. So, Tuesday afternoon a small light plane circled the snow-clad mountain and David's ashes were cast free to rest among the peaks forever.

My mom was twelve when her brother died. At some point, she stapled her own account of the tragedy to the newspaper clipping.

I was the one to know first. Pam and I were going to go swimming, and we had just walked out of the house. The phone rang, I answered, said Mother wasn't home, and wrote down the message—to call Emergency Operator number 62.

Pam was my best friend and had been since the second

grade. We shared so much together, all the delights and disappointments of tomboys. But she made me very mad that day. She kept insisting that I hurry up, and I couldn't because I knew something was wrong—I even knew with whom.

Mommy came home right then, and I told Pam to go on and I would catch up after I gave her the message. Oh, I was so afraid. I just sat on the steps and waited. Poor Mommy, she just folded down on her knees and covered her face and said, "Dear God, no." I ran in and tried to hold her but she wouldn't let me. So I said, "David's really alright," and she ran into the bedroom. I knew he wasn't. I knew he was dead.

The phone was just dangling, so I picked it up and said, "David's alright now"—and the man said, "God, I'm sorry. Can you give me your father's number?" Mommy came out of the bedroom right after I hung up and got mad at me for telling them Daddy's office number. And she quickly called him, told him not to answer any more calls but to get home immediately.

He was my only brother, you see, and he and Daddy were so very close. Mommy didn't even hold me then, and I got scared thinking about what would happen when Daddy got home, so I got my book and went out to the woods to read. I did too—Wild Animals I Have Known by Ernest Thompson Seton. I read about a cougar, a badger, and a bear.

Then I heard Daddy calling me across the pond so I went home. He was sitting on the rattan stool with his back against the wall, looking up at the ceiling and crying. Mommy was across from him in the soft chair with her head resting in her hands. I sat down on the hearth, and Daddy said, "Your *brother has been killed in an avalanche with six other boys. Now, you don't have to see your friends or you may want to. They will know about it because it will be in the papers."*

Then he got on the phone and called all the relatives and my sister who was away at camp. I went and sat on the bed in David's room and listened to what Daddy was saying. He asked my sister if she wanted to come home and she didn't. And he asked Mommy's mother to come up and help. And he told his father, "David's gone, Dad. Yup. It was an avalanche—six other boys caught too. Hmm-hmm. It was the way he would have wanted it. You know how he loved the mountains—we must be thankful for that. No, Dad, I'm going to fly out there tomorrow and see what I can find out. Their group leader didn't get caught but he's been hospitalized for shock."

Later, Mommy said she didn't believe in God anymore. I cried myself to sleep, trying to bury myself into the mattress and find something of David.

Daddy was already gone when I woke up the next morning. Mommy was still asleep but there was a lot of noise from somewhere. I went to the kitchen and the noise became voices from the garage. So I looked out, and there were all our neighbors and friends standing in the garage and out in the driveway. They all had dark colors on and some had armloads of food. The enormous ham on the kitchen table registered then. The Deans were our immediate neighbors, and David, my sister, and I loved them very much. I ran to Harriet who was coming to me, and for the first time I cried because David was dead, and not because he wasn't there to make me happy when Daddy and Mommy were being so strange.

Harriet comforted me and said everyone should come in and have some coffee. Mommy came out then and oh, she looked so terrible. Betty Mathews, her best friend, comforted her and told her she didn't have to worry about a thing. There was enough food for a week, and the reporters had already come and been told where to go in no uncertain terms. The telephone had been turned over to an answering service that wouldn't let any calls but family ones get through. Mommy said she would have gotten out the guns if she had seen the press people.

I went to stay with my friend Pam and her parents. I stayed there two weeks and found out what happened through the papers. I went home occasionally, but Mommy had fallen down and broken a tooth and was in too much pain to say much.

I only cried once the whole time, and that was when I saw Life *magazine. They had pictures of the bodies being carried down the mountain on mules. I am horrified now by the idea that I could see such a thing. I was twelve years old, and I saw a bunch of canvas sacks draped over mules. And I knew one of those sacks was my brother.*

I want to go back in time and hug that twelve-year-old girl in the wake of her brother's death. This voice of my mother, young and vulnerable, one that I have never heard, breaks my heart. I see her sitting on the hearth as her father tells her that her brother is gone forever. I feel her world darken and close in around her. I want to catch her from falling. But it's too late. How can someone endure such a loss and come out of it healed?

If my mom hadn't lost her brother, David, she *would* have been a different person. Maybe she would have been able to cope with the challenges of being a mother. Maybe her mother wouldn't have drunk herself to death. I cross into that forbidden landscape of what would happen to me if I lost one of my children. I'd drink myself dead too. I wish that just once I could be brave enough to let down my guard and give myself permission to be the girl who throws herself across her mother's body and weeps. What will it take for me to break? To fall down and admit how truly scared I am of her leaving this time?

NOW

some kind of trust

I turn on the heat in the rental car and call my husband in tears. "I don't know what I'm doing here," I tell him.

"It's alright. You can stay as long as you need to," he says gently.

"No, I can't. I don't want to. I promised Dominic and Bella I'd be back for New Year's."

"We're okay, really," he assures me.

In sixteen years, my husband, Anthony, and I have never been apart on New Year's Eve. On our first New Year's Eve together, we hopped into his '66 Bonneville at a quarter to midnight and drove along the Pacific Coast Highway searching for an unpopulated stretch of sand. We parked in the darkness and listened to the surf pound the shore for a few moments. Then we stripped off all our clothes and ran toward the water. We ran full speed, naked, hand in hand into the Pacific Ocean.

We held on to each other in the deep water and stared up at the huge, pale moon over us. My body was shaking, the water moving all around us in swells. I was fearful of the ocean—always dreaming of drowning in the waves. But in those seconds,

I felt safe like I never had before. I trusted his arms around me. I think I trusted the whole universe.

We galloped back through the surf and onto the sand, bitterly cold and laughing. We had emerged from the Pacific Ocean and into the beginning of the new year, baptized and restored.

God, I miss that kind of trust in myself. I need the girl willing to jump in the ocean at midnight right now. I need to believe that water will keep me afloat. A lodestar, the briny ocean, the giant moon, and the faith that I am safe.

My husband helped me through some difficult years when we were first dating. He was making the rounds as an actor in Los Angeles, and I was studying to get my undergraduate degree at UCLA. I'd sometimes fall into uncontrollable crying spells, even though I was happy and deeply in love with him.

"What's wrong?" he'd ask.

"I don't know," I'd always reply.

I didn't want him to know that there were feelings inside me that were frightening and had no explanation. I didn't want him to know that I was leavable.

I remember him holding my shoulders and looking into my eyes, "You are a *good* person, Melissa. An *inherently* good person, and you matter in this world. Do you understand that?"

These words were unbearable. I fought them. I told him he was wrong, that I was not a good person. I was damaged inside.

"Inherently good," he said over and over, until I began to trust that he wasn't was going to change his mind and walk out on me.

I still need him to teach me how a family stays together—no matter what happens.

"We'll be waiting for you," he tells me before hanging up.

I exhale. These are the moments when I feel lucky in love.

I start up the engine and drive toward downtown. I'm anxious about traveling too far from the house in case anything goes wrong while I'm gone.

I stop at the gas-station market and buy a roll of butter rum Life Savers and two scratch-off lottery tickets. My mom always wanted to win the lottery. In fact, she's counted on it. Years ago, she insisted that when she hit the big jackpot, she was going to buy me a horse that could jump the moon. Then she was going to get her face lifted and eyes done. She and I would go to a pricey resort where we would sip on fancy drinks served in pineapples and have our toenails painted at the same time. Winning the lottery was going to change her life.

She's awake when I get back, lying on her side with Sparky and her other dog, Trinket, nestled behind her knees.

I hand her a ticket.

Then I realize that her fingers can't manage the scratch-off part.

"I'll do it for you, Mom."

"Thanks, darlin'."

I scratch her ticket until my thumbnail turns grimy. "Nothing this time," I tell her. I feel foolish for buying her a lottery ticket. She's never going to win.

I scratch my ticket. It's a two-dollar instant winner.

"You've always been the lucky one," she says to me. "You got that luck of the Irish from your dad."

She's right about this. My father never failed to remind us that we came from a family of Irish storytellers and that luck and blarney ran deep in our roots.

THEN

rabbit-rabbit

Last night my father crept into my room and told me he was going to die. I didn't believe him. It's hard these days to know what is true. But I am wiser now about the comings and goings of people from our big yellow house, since I started seventh grade. I have my own AM-FM alarm clock radio. My clock radio has bright red neon numbers that you can see in the dark, a turn dial for both AM and FM radio, and an eleven-minute snooze button. It stays next to my bed and helps me keep track of everyone. Last night when my dad came in and sat on the end of my bed, it was exactly 2:14.

I heard his truck coming down the gravel road first, and then saw the quick flash of headlights through my bedroom window. My dad's truck bumps the loudest over the potholes and always pulls up to the same spot underneath the bay laurel tree. The engine lulls for a moment, then lets out a series of sputters like the coughing sounds my brother makes when he wants to stay home from school. Even from the way the heavy door slams shut, I know it is my dad's white Ford truck.

I looked over at my clock radio, saw the lined binder paper

lying on top of it, and remembered that it was a Rabbit-Rabbit night. Before falling asleep, I made a sign with big red-ink letters to remind myself to say the words "Rabbit-Rabbit" before I say anything else when I wake up. If I say "Rabbit-Rabbit" as soon as I wake up in the morning on the first day of the new month, I will have good luck all month.

I forgot to say "Rabbit-Rabbit" the last two months, and that's when the raccoons got back into the barn and killed two more chickens, and Tracy Dunn shoved me into the oleander bushes for no reason at all. Now my mom's canceled her trip to come visit us, and I am sure it had something to do with my forgetting two months in a row.

As I listen to my dad's footsteps coming up the stairs, it's clear that I need to stick to the Rabbit-Rabbit plan, that I really need to go back to sleep—that I need some good luck.

When the hall light clicks on, my dad is standing in my bedroom doorway. A bright yellow halo backlights him.

"Melissa. Wake up," he says.

I don't say anything. I pretend to be asleep. He comes to my bed and sits down heavily, as if to bounce me awake.

"You have to get up," he says more urgently.

I peek at the red numbers of my clock radio. Two fourteen.

His voice is muffled and he says, "You've got to help me."

I open one eye: he is holding a white rag over his mouth and nose. For a moment, I think that he is crying.

"What are you doing, Dad?" I finally say.

"I'm going to die," he says.

It's quiet for a minute, with the exception of our dog, Amy, lapping water out of the toilet bowl in the bathroom.

"I'm going to die if it happens again," he says.

"If what happens?" I say.

He starts telling me the whole story.

"I was driving home and it started. I couldn't stop it. I sneezed and sneezed, and I counted the sneezes. I sneezed *eight* times in row. Do you know what happens to you if you sneeze nine times in a row? *You die*."

He gestures to his white rag. "I'm trying to hold it in."

"Dad, I have never heard that."

"Everybody knows this," he says.

"Is it some sort of Irish thing?" I ask.

"It's not Irish. It's just a *thing* everybody knows. If you sneeze nine times in a row, you will die. If I die, I need you to be the one to tell people what happened."

I look at my dad with his shoulders hunched and that white rag pushed into his face, and I try to make sense of everything he is saying. But I am too smart to fall for this. The time on my clock radio confirms it. I know the Bit-a-Honey downtown stays open until two in the morning. I even know what he orders when he's out—Myers's rum with Coke and a slice of lime. If I were with him, he would order me a Shirley Temple with two cherries.

"Go to bed, Dad. It's a school night and you've been drinking rum," I tell him.

He doesn't move from the end of my bed. He sits there like he didn't even hear me.

Then he raises his voice at me. "How dare you! I'm going to die and you don't even care. You're going to be sorry!"

I lie very still as he says these things. He needs comfort

or sympathy or something from me. I am not going to give it to him.

He stands. "I can't believe you, of all people…" He exits my room, his white rag held desperately to his face.

I listen carefully as he moves around the house. In the kitchen he tells our dog, Amy, his story. But mostly he tells her about me, about how I don't care enough about him to even get up and be with him in his last moments. He tells her that "of all people," I should be the one to understand.

My thoughts jump around like firecrackers exploding on the pavement. It occurs to me that I may be wrong. Is it possible that if you sneeze nine times in a row you can die? I have never sneezed more than three times in a row. Why did he have the rag? Should I be doing something to help him? And how much later could the ninth sneeze come?

I force my eyes closed, but my mind stays awake. I try counting sheep and goats, but it doesn't work. I wonder if I should get up and check on my dad.

───────

I wake first thing in the morning with a sick feeling, like I've eaten something bad. I don't even look at my clock radio because I'm thinking about what happened last night. I am the one who is supposed to wake up my dad on school mornings, but I am afraid. The house is still quiet. And it's cold. So cold that I pull on my red parka over my clothes. I walk with my arms tightly wrapped around myself and stand at the foot of the attic stairs.

"Dad! Time to get up!" I yell.

"Dad! Dad! Dad?" I yell three more times.

He usually says, "Okay."

I have a feeling now that something is very wrong. I panic and begin to climb the staircase to his room, passing the strange painting of dark-skinned natives pushing a boat out from a riverbank. "Boris," the head of the wild boar my dad shot and had stuffed, juts out of the wall at the top of the stairs. As my toes touch the top stair, I notice for the first time just how many antique tools, blades, and implements are hanging on the wall. I keep my eyes focused on the wall of gadgets and say, "Dad. It's time to get up."

When he doesn't answer, I turn and see his body piled up with striped wool blankets. *He told me I would be sorry…He told me he might die.*

Nothing makes sense. I glance down, afraid to take in the stillness of his body. There on his bedside table are scattered coins, gum wrappers, Excedrin tablets, and an antique bottle embossed with the words "The Waters of Life."

"DAD!" I yell as loud as I can.

His body stirs ever so slightly. He lifts a blanket from his face and squints at me with bloodshot eyes.

"Don't ever do that again!" I yell. But my voice is shaking. My whole body is shaking. I have never yelled at him before.

He smiles at me. It is a cheery leprechaun smile.

"It's not funny, Dad!"

"It's too early to get up," he mumbles and pulls the wool blanket over his head.

How could he do that to me? I want him to understand how

confusing it is to live in this house sometimes. I am so mad at him, but I can't think of the right words so I stand for a minute thinking of what else to say. Something gathers in my throat and I am about to say it but I can't.

I turn away.

I leave him there in his messed-up bed, and as I walk down the stairs, I remember something truly terrible.

I didn't say, "Rabbit-Rabbit." The one thing I wanted to do right.

I kick my math book across the linoleum floor.

I don't care. It's a stupid thing anyway. Like saying "Rabbit-Rabbit" is going to change anything in our yellow house. It's not going to change how much my dad drinks at the Bit-a-Honey or stop the raccoons from killing our chickens late at night or make my brothers any nicer to me. And it's certainly not going to make our mom get on a plane and visit us.

NOW

strike three

I set my winning lottery ticket on her bedside table. What's so lucky about winning two dollars in the lottery when I'm going to lose my mom forever?

She asks for a sip of water, and this time I know how to hold the straw for her. I tear open the roll of butter rum Life Savers and offer her one.

"I brought you a Life Saver, Mom." I quickly realize it's a pretty stupid gesture because she can't eat.

"Mmm, what flavor is it?" she asks. Her eyes are closing.

"Butter rum."

"Yee-uck," she says.

I thought she liked butter rum. But it's me who likes butter rum. Two strikes. A losing lottery ticket and a flavor she hates.

I want to say something meaningful to her while she's still awake. I'm reaching for something profound or bigger than both of us, but I can't form the words. Everything feels too late to say. If I had an ounce of courage, I would reach out and rest my hand on her warm forehead. But I'm a water skeeter darting and skimming the surface of a lake I am afraid to swim in. Facing her and her imminent death is the collision of the past, the present, and the future all at once. What can I say to her that's at least familiar? I glance at the lottery ticket, and of all things, a pony gallops into my mind.

"Mom, remember when we drove Jackson across country from Vermont to California?"

She opens one eye and looks around the room. "Jackson? Who's Jackson?"

How could she forget about Jackson? The horse she once put all her faith in.

Strike three.

THEN

getting to california

I'm having second thoughts about having bought that pony," says my mom.

"Yeah. He hates being in the trailer," I say.

"It's the gasoline too. Costing me a goddamn fortune pulling a trailer."

Jamie, me, my mom, and the pony have been on the road for five days, traveling across country in my mom's red Datsun. She bought the pony for three hundred dollars and plans to train him and then sell him for a high price. She offered to take us on her trip from Vermont to California before school starts so that we could have some extra time to visit with her. I'll be starting junior high in eight days. She says she will drop us off in California and then head home to Washington with the pony. This trip means I get to spend a whole extra week with my mom.

My dad was hesitant about the road trip, but I begged him to say yes and reminded him that we could always call from pay phones along the way. Eden had no interest in road traveling and got an invitation to stay at his friend's house for the week.

The pony named Jackson in the trailer behind us has been

nothing but trouble since we left. He refuses to get back into the trailer when we let him out to stretch his legs, and it can take anywhere from a few minutes to a few hours to lure him back in. We had to tether him to a tree for the night in Nebraska when we heard on the radio that a tornado was ripping through the plains. We'd huddled in the Datsun, with the rain threatening to pierce the metal roof, and watched Jackson through the blur of the downpour. He stayed perfectly still with his hind end to the wind and his head bent down low, as the lightning lit up the whole field around him. My mom decided then and there that he probably had some wild Mustang in him.

"He's got character and potential," says my mom. "That's why I bought him. If I can get him trained, he could be a champion show pony someday and worth a hell of a lot of money."

This is the first horse my mom has ever owned.

"Maybe you can be the one to show him someday," my mom says to me.

My whole body turns into a field of goose bumps. I'd love nothing more. I'm getting to be a really strong rider, and my mom tells me that I have good hands and a natural seat. She should know: she grew up riding at the prestigious Ox Ridge Hunt Club in Darien, Connecticut. We share this deep love of horses and riding.

"Madison Square Garden, here we come!" she hollers out the window.

Right now though, we're just trying to get to California as fast as possible so we won't have to get Jackson in and out of the trailer again. My mom had me crawl in the trailer at the last stop to check his legs and make sure there was no heat or swelling from standing in the trailer too long.

On this trip, I have seen more cornfields, cars, and cows than I ever could have imagined. I sit in the front seat and Jamie mostly sleeps stretched out in the back. Like Jackson, he's not a very good traveler. He said to wake him up when we get to California. Not me; I'd rather stay awake the whole way and see as much as I can.

Late at night is the best time to drive. There's a hum to the road, a music-like sound that comes from the tires moving fast along the pavement. We pass trucks as big as whales and trailers full of cows and pigs and chickens and corn. On the opposite side of the highway, I track the headlights in the distance as they zoom toward us like bright comets and then disappear. And then there are the bumps in the road that remind us to stay awake and drive another hundred miles.

My mom tells me, "Go to sleep, darling."

"But you need me to keep you awake," I remind her.

"Nah, I've got pills for that. Just try to close your eyes."

But I want to stay awake forever. The August night is full of winking stars, and I love the hum and roll of the road all night long. I want to sit next to her until the sky turns lavender.

"Crawl in back and get some sleep," my mom says, sounding tired and edgy.

I can tell she wants to be alone in the night. I think she likes the dark quiet as much as I do. We are from the same family of barn owls, I suppose. I lift my knees and curl my toes against the warm dashboard.

"I'm just not tired, Mom."

Maybe it's because I've got her all to myself and there's nowhere to go except straight ahead. The white stripes and yellow dashes on the pavement could take us to so many places together.

"I always wanted to be a truck driver," she tells me.

"Yeah, me too," I say.

She turns and looks at me like she doesn't believe me.

"I think I'd like the life," she says as she cracks her window open to let the smoke from her cigarette trail outside. "I'd even like to write a book on all the best trucker diners to stop at," she says.

It's true; she is very particular about where we stop. If she sees a lot of big hauling trucks parked outside a diner, we pull over. We sit at the counter along with all the truckers. My mom tells me that real truckers can be the most fascinating people. She smiles and stirs her coffee in circles when she talks to them and then always asks them the same question: "Where you headed?" She waits for them to ask her the same question in return but sometimes they don't.

Back in Iowa, while Jamie and I were spinning around on the counter seats, the long-haired trucker next to us told my mom that he'd like to take her all the way across the country sitting on his lap. She sat up especially tall, threw her head back, and laughed. When we returned to the car, she was all giddy. She rolled down the windows and cranked up the radio.

Tonight, we pass a bright pink neon sign along the roadside. "MOTEL, MOTEL," it blinks. My eyes itch when I look at it. I'd like to stay in that motel with the flashing sign. But we're not staying in motels on this trip; we're sleeping in the Datsun. My dad thinks we're staying overnight in motels, but he doesn't know all the details about traveling with a difficult pony like Jackson. Besides, truck drivers don't stay in motels. My mom says they have wonderful beds right inside their trucks and don't need to stay in a motel or inn, so neither do we. "MOTEL, MOTEL," stay awake, stay awake—that's the last thing I remember.

My mom shakes my shoulder back and forth. "Melissa!" she says. It hurts to open my eyes in the brightness. My cheek is pressed hard between the window and the metal door handle. I squint out through the windshield, mad that I fell asleep. I was supposed to stay up all night.

"Look out your window," she says.

I turn my head. There are hundreds of them. No, thousands. "What are they?"

"Antelope," she whispers.

I whisper the word "antelope" because I know they might disappear, that I might be dreaming this. There are miles of them. Everything in sight is blue sky, golden grass, and antelope.

"Where are we?"

"Wyoming," my mom says.

I decide here and now that Wyoming is my favorite place. Even Jamie wakes up to see the antelope fields and says it's almost as good as watching *Wild Kingdom* on Sunday nights. For miles we watch the herds of grazing antelope.

When the antelope are far behind us, we pull into a diner for my mom's coffee. Behind the counter, mounted on the wall, I see the head of a rabbit with a set of antlers alongside its long ears. The small gold plaque underneath it reads "Wyoming's Famous Jackalope."

"What the heck?" I say out loud. The man behind the counter asks me if I've ever seen one.

"I saw a lot of antelope on the way here," I say.

"Yeah, those jackalope are hard to see. You got to watch the fields real careful. They're quick little nippers."

Wyoming is getting better by the second.

"Gas is goddamn expensive here," says my mom. She makes a face into her Styrofoam cup. "And the coffee is crap too."

I take it to mean that this is not a good truck stop.

We don't get breakfast at the diner. Instead, we walk across the street to a grocery store. Jamie hands my mom a big bag of potato chips and a handful of black licorice ropes.

"No," she says. "We're getting two things here. Bread and orange cheese."

"That's just stupid," says Jamie.

"Well, that's all we can afford," she says.

"I'm going back to the car," Jamie says, walking away.

Mom grabs him by the T-shirt. "Look, we've got forty-two dollars to get from here to California, and we can't get there without fuel in the tank. *Capiche?*"

I watch my mom from the rearview mirror as she pumps gas into the tank. The Wyoming wind blows her curly hair in all directions. From the backseat Jamie says, "You notice we're not skimping on coffee and cigarettes. God no, not that. I say Mom ought to unhitch this trailer and turn that mule out with the antelope where it belongs."

"Don't be a jerk. Jackson is not a mule," I say.

I gaze out the window all day searching for a jackalope. My mom made a good decision about the orange cheese. It is the best cheese I have ever tasted, and I tell her over and over how much I like it. It's creamy and fat and tastes good smashed against the soft, white bread. I tell her it's better than any truck-stop meal.

I close my eyes at the worst time. When I open them, my mom is pulling over to the side of the road. I turn around to check if there's a police car.

"Why are we stopping here?" Jamie asks, popping up from the backseat.

My mom reaches across me and rolls down the window. A tall, scruffy man is standing outside the car. He has on blue jeans, with a tie-dyed bandanna around his head and a knapsack on his back.

"Where you headed?" she yells.

"Grantsville, Utah," he says, looking into our small car. "Just outside Salt Lake."

It's not fair. Now she's doing what she said she wasn't going to do.

"I need someone to help with the driving," she says.

"Yeah, I can do that," he says.

She avoids my eyes, but I see my mom thinking for a second. That's her judgment second, when she decides if she's going to say, "Sorry, man—we're not going that far," or, "Hop in." She promised us that we were not going to pick up hitchhikers on this trip. She told us she only picks up hitchhikers if they live locally. This guy does not look local to me. I glance at Jamie who must have been sleeping too. He would have grabbed the steering wheel if he had seen her trying to pull over to pick some guy up.

"Melissa, hop in the backseat," she says.

"This is bull," says Jamie.

The tall man takes my front seat and then adjusts it back to make room for his long legs. He smells like salty soup and chewing tobacco.

While my mom drives, she and the stranger talk. I get the details. His name is Frank, and he's going to Utah to get a job because he's "flat broke." He says he's been hanging out on the road trying to get a hitch for the last three hours.

"Good thing you came along," he says, grinning back at me.

Yeah, good for him. He asks her for a cigarette, and together they smoke and talk in the front seat. She tells him about her champion pony back in the trailer.

The next time we pull over, it is late at night and my mom gets into the passenger seat. She wraps a blanket around herself and closes her eyes while she talks. She tells him that she hasn't slept in days, and that she still has two states to go after she drops us off in California.

"Maybe I'll stick around in California with my pony for a little while," she tells him.

I wonder if that means longer than a week. I pretend to be asleep. Then I open my eyes like a wide-eyed owl and watch the back of Frank's head. I will watch the back of his head until the daylight comes. I watch the shadow of his dark curly beard, the curve of his sharp nose, the outline of his lips, and the white edge of his eye. His hands, covered in a pair of gray socks with holes cut out for the thumbs, rest on top of the steering wheel.

I hate him for being in our car, for being in charge of our car.

I'm mad at my mom for lying. This was supposed to be a family trip. I figure at this point he can pretty much take us down any road he wants and I won't know the difference because these roads all look the same. I take notes in my mind of the exit numbers on the green-and-white road signs. I keep myself awake by looking for jackalopes in the dark until we pass a sign that says, "Now leaving Wyoming." My chances of sighting a jackalope are shot.

I suppose her judgment was all right, because Frank doesn't fall asleep while driving or take us to some strange deserted road to kill us or steal our car. When we pull onto the Grantsville overpass he thanks us for the ride, then asks my mom if she "could spare a little cash."

"Honey, I don't even have the money to make it to California." She reaches into her bag and hands him a cigarette.

When Frank asks for that cash loan, Jamie covers his mouth like he's coughing, but he starts laughing so hard into his hand that he can't stop. I don't get it. Then Jamie leans over to me and whispers, "It's the poor asking the poor." Then he starts laughing even harder. And I laugh too, because his laugh sounds so good to me. It's a sound I haven't heard in a long time.

When Frank steps out of the car, my mom says, "Melissa, hop in the front seat."

The left blinker click-clicks.

"That's okay, Mom. I think I'll stay in the back."

I turn around to look at the tan-and-white horse trailer still behind us. I hope that Jackson's legs aren't starting to swell from being in the trailer for too long. I'm tired and I'm sick of the orange cheese. Right now, nothing sounds better than getting to California. And nothing feels better than seeing things from Jamie's point of view in the backseat.

———

When we run out of money in Nevada, my mom calls my dad. He has an old college friend meet us down at the Boomtown Reno all-you-can-eat buffet to loan us some cash. My mom says we can "go all out." Jamie and I fill our plates like pig troughs. Green Jell-O cubes, layers of pink roast beef, scoops of mashed potatoes, tropical fruit salad, chocolate pudding, and gooey spare ribs that hang over the edges of our plates. We eat like we haven't eaten in weeks.

My mom has a few glasses of wine and fills a thermos with coffee before we get back on the road. I try to convince her to let me play the nickel slots. I might get lucky in Boomtown. I could win us all the money we need to get home. But she says no, her luck was just fine. There was still Jackson, after all, waiting in the trailer.

THEN

running on empty

Aweek later, two ladies are walking down our gravel road in high heels. Both wear black skirts and have canvas bags hanging off their shoulders. One has a lavender-colored shirt tucked in at the waist. The other one wears a plain white-collared shirt. Strangers don't usually come down our long gravel road unless they're lost, and especially not in high heels on a Saturday morning. I tell my mom to take a look out the window.

"Born-agains," she says.

"What do you mean by 'born-agains'?"

"Religious people. They go door to door trying to save you."

"Save you from what?"

She laughs. "Your soul landing in hell, I suppose."

My mom snips at her fingernails with a pair of metal clippers. The little crescents, still painted pink, fly up and skitter across the kitchen floor. A cigarette dangles from her mouth like a lollipop stick.

"They'll try to tell you what you should believe in. You can talk to them if you want, but I'm busy packing up," she says.

I want to run and shut the front door quickly, but I hear heels clunking up the wooden stairs like heavy, tired horses. Then a voice echoes into the house, "Hello in there. Anybody home?"

"I don't want them to talk to me," I say. "Can't you, Mom, please?"

"Oh no," she says. "If you don't want to talk to them, then you tell them that. And don't be a pip-squeak, for Pete's sake."

"Hello," says the voice on the porch.

I run my tongue along my teeth, still gritty from not having been brushed this morning. I half-slip on my navy Keds and shuffle toward the front door. I suppose I can say that I'm on the way out to do my chores and that I don't have time to talk.

"Well, good morning. Aren't you a pretty one?" says the lady in lavender with a huge smile. "What's your name?"

"Melissa," I tell her.

"Melissa. Now that's a pretty name. I don't think we have ever met such a pretty girl with that name. Have we, Lila Jane?"

Lila Jane, in white, smiles and shakes her head no. She's got her hair pulled up tight in a skinny ponytail and has orange freckles splattered across her face. Her eyes are blue like mine and we have the same middle name, though I never tell anyone that's my middle name unless they really want to know. She shifts from foot to foot like she's a little bit nervous.

Ruth, in the lavender, introduces herself and then starts talking on and on like she's never going to stop. She talks about God, the King of Endless Glory, the Power of Faith, sin, salvation, and a lot of other things I don't understand. I just nod my head a lot in the same way that Lila Jane does. I'm mostly interested in the color of her shirt, because it's not really lavender now that I'm taking a closer look at it. It's lilac, just like the old-fashioned lilacs that grow in our garden every spring.

Finally, Ruth pauses and says, "Have you ever been to church, sweetie?"

"No, not really," I say.

"Well, we don't want to overwhelm you, but we would like to talk with you some more and leave you some of our *lit-ra-ture*."

She hands me a thin paper booklet from out of her canvas bag. On the cover is a picture of a man who looks like he's drowning in a river. His hands are up in the air, his chin is halfway underwater, and he definitely looks like he wants to be saved. I guess this is what my mom was talking about.

"Do you like stories?" asks Lila Jane.

The one called Ruth peers past me and through the doorway. Like me, she hears the teakettle whistling in the kitchen. Then it stops whistling.

"Is that your mom in the kitchen?" she asks.

"Oh yeah. She's just visiting. She lives in Washington. You know, the state."

Ruth looks at Lila Jane, then back at me. "Well, give her a holler. We'd like to give her some *lit-ra-ture* also," she finally says.

I yell for my mom to come because I'm not sure why she didn't want to talk with them in the first place. The ladies really are friendly.

My mom takes her time getting to the door, and I'm glad when she shows up without a cigarette in her mouth. She politely nods when Ruth gives her the same big, warm smile and starts talking about believing in God and the Endless Glory and all that.

I step sideways so that I can watch my mom's face closely.

Maybe these ladies are different from the born-agains she was telling me about. My mom keeps listening intently, then suddenly interrupts Ruth.

"Well, that's all very nice, but I believe in other things."

"Would you mind me asking you a question?" Ruth says.

"Certainly not."

"What it is that you believe in, *really believe* in?"

It is a good question, but I sure am glad she didn't ask me. I wouldn't know what to say. I turn and look at my mom, and a shiver suddenly goes all the way up the back of my legs. *I'm going to find out what my mom really believes in.*

My mom straightens her whole body, making herself a good two inches taller. She places her hands on her hips like she's posing for a magazine cover.

"You know what I believe in?" She points to the half-acre pasture outside our house. "You see that pony out there?"

We all turn and look. There is Jackson, the crazy dappled-gray pony my mom hauled out here from Vermont a week ago.

"*That's* what I believe in. That pony is going to be a champion someday."

For a second, I think she is going to say something more. But I look at her eyes—serious, focused, and absolutely certain of what she believes in: Jackson.

Nobody says anything. We just stare at Jackson with his head down, yanking up mouthfuls of grass and swishing his tail back and forth at the flies.

"In fact, darlin'," my mom says to me, "that champion-to-be pony hasn't been fed this morning. Why don't you run out and give him some hay."

"We'll just leave this booklet for you anyway," Ruth says to my mom.

"That won't be necessary," she says.

I'm starting down the stairs when Ruth adds, "Why don't we walk out with you? Love to get a closer look at that pony."

The ladies follow me out to the pasture in their high heels. I tell them to watch out for the piles of manure. They talk about the God stuff but Lila Jane asks me a lot of questions about Jackson, like maybe she's starting to believe in him too. I tell her how Jackson almost ended up in the glue factory, but my mom saved him. I tell her how he is a really crazy pony, but that's only because he was beaten up by this horse dealer that sold him to my mom.

"That's awful," says Lila Jane.

"Yeah, she had to pay three hundred dollars for him. And then she found out that he hates getting in the trailer so that's been a problem in getting him places."

Lila Jane shakes her head.

"And the farrier charges an extra forty dollars to nail shoes on Jackson because he's a kicker and needs to be tied down and sedated."

Jackson looks up at us with his ears perked forward and tosses his head in a playful sort of way.

"The thing is, he can sometimes be the sweetest pony ever."

The first time my mom saw Jackson, she fell in love with his big glassy eyes and dark gray dapples. Then she found out that this pony could jump a four-foot fence from a standstill. She says he may be scared out of his mind, but he's got heart. That's where the champion part comes in. My mom says that, with some training, he could be a top pony jumper—maybe even get to Madison Square Garden someday. She named him Jackson for short, but his real name—his show name—is "Running on Empty." It's her favorite song by Jackson Browne.

I love his dark gray dapples too. But I'm not so sure about Jackson Running on Empty. I don't trust him when I give him his grain. Sometimes he's just fine, but other times he turns sour and corners me with his ears flat and his nostrils flared. He's kicked me hard too. And he *can* jump four feet from a standstill, but it's usually because he's trying to escape.

Lila Jane says she always wanted a horse. Ruth asks me if it would be all right for them to come back sometime soon. I want to say no. But I say, "I don't know," instead. I wish I could come up with an answer the way my mom does. I wish I had something to believe in like that—*really believe* in—even if it were just a dappled gray pony named Running on Empty.

I watch Ruth and Lila disappear around the bend of our long driveway. Maybe they won't return like they said they would. People don't always keep their promises. I walk into the kitchen and sit across from my mom's blue duffel bag. She is always leaving. I don't know when I will see her next. Maybe Jackson won't turn out the way she hopes, and she'll come back and live with us. There's always that chance.

NOW

real soon, sugar

As I sit here beside my fading mother, I understand that Jackson was but a brief passing fancy in her life, and yet he seemed like everything to her at the time. Jackson was supposed to change her life. He was her winning lottery ticket. And I wanted to believe in him too. The ladies never came back, and I never went to church once until I met my husband. Thinking about it now, my mom really did put all her faith in that horse. One of her letters reminds me.

Dear Melissa,

I am having the most difficult time deciding what to do. Sure wish you were around so you could help me see things from a clear perspective. I do think that I might stay here for the winter if I can find a job right quick. If this pony Jackson turns out to be the high-priced article we expect him to be—well, I could be in really decent financial shape by the time summer is underway. I don't want to keep being away from you—Oy, it is difficult. I wish that you could be here. Though I don't think I could get myself to leave Jackson. He will be my nest egg, on top of being my very good friend and companion. He's been wonderful other than his blasted hind feet that are so long they are interfering with his proper movement and putting too much strain on his pasterns and tendons. Please let me hear from you real soon, Sugar. I want to know how you are feeling about things too— not just news. God, I miss you.

She believed in that pony until it became apparent that Jackson was actually a little nutty and didn't have the temperament to be a "champion." As I watch my mom drifting out of this life, I wonder what she really believes in now. What stopped her from putting her faith in us instead?

NOW

bleeding

There is a pool of deep red blood on the bathroom floor and a trail of smudged prints leading out of the bathroom. I feel queasy as I stare at the blood. It's infected. Hepatitis blood. My mom's blood. Kim explains that my mom didn't have a good night and that she stepped on a piece of glass when she was in the bathroom. He had to make sure that he stopped the bleeding since her blood has very little clotting ability at this point. I know that the veins surrounding her diseased liver are engorged like fat sausages stuffed into thin casings. If these veins give out and burst, she will internally bleed to death very quickly. This detail has been nagging me because it can't be seen.

I want to do the right thing and offer to clean the blood off the bathroom floor, but I chicken out and back slowly out of the room. I'm uneasy around blood. I can still see Eden's face covered in blood when he and Jamie got in a rock fight with some kids on the back hill. I remember once cutting my pet chicken's toenail too short and blood spurting out. I recall the sharp taste of blood pooling in my mouth after Eden slugged me in the face for hogging the heat on our old floor heater. And then there was the kind of blood that I needed to hide.

THEN

pee-chees

I am bleeding too much. We are out of paper towels in the kitchen. We are out of Zee napkins in the pantry. The art of my carefully folded and scotch-taped toilet paper is no longer working. I cut my white PE tube socks into rectangular strips and shove them down into my underwear.

I lie down on my bedroom floor and reach my arm underneath my dresser. I reach all the way back until I feel the baseboard and then hop my hand around until I feel the small green wallet I keep hidden from my brothers—who have taken to stealing things from my room. I open it to see how much money I have. Not certain how much I need, I take all of the neatly folded bills, slide them into the pocket of my jeans, then adjust the rectangular sock strips.

I get on my ten-speed and race down Center Road. I really can't stand these fat socks between my legs. I wish I didn't live in a house of boys. It's becoming harder to keep secrets. As I pedal, I make the mistake of looking up. Walking toward me are Emily Fink and Laura Lee West in their matching Dittos jeans. Shit. Of all the stupid people in this whole town, it has to be Emily Fink.

Laura Lee is all right, but a year and a half ago in sixth-grade health class, when we were about to see "the Movie" called *Growing Up and Liking It*, Emily Fink announced, "I can't wait to see Melissa's face when she sees this." Then she turned to Laura Lee and said about me, "She's so immature."

I didn't have a clue what having a period was, and it stunned and embarrassed me. Throughout the movie, all I could think about was what Emily Fink had said and what my face should or should not look like. Then there was that awful moment when the movie ended and all the fluorescent lights flooded the room. Emily Fink, with her perfectly flipped hair, was staring at me.

"So what did you think?" she asked.

I wanted to be casual. "About what?"

"Duh, about the movie."

"Oh yeah. I already knew about all that stuff."

"Yeah, right. Why is your face so red then?"

I wanted to punch her right then and there. But she was a foot taller than me and had breasts already.

It would be too obvious if I swerved my bike to the other side of the street just to avoid Emily Fink. So I push my head down, focusing on the blur of the spokes, and pedal as fast as I can. I hear Laura Lee say, "Hi," but I race right by, pretending that I don't even see them.

I turn my bike toward Longs Drugs. I *hate* going into Longs because I got caught changing price tags there when I was ten. Jamie showed me the tag-changing trick when we were over at TG&Y after school, and I thought it was a perfectly good idea. I spent a lot of time wandering around in Longs and deciding what would be a fair price for items. I didn't try to hide it; I just peeled off stickers and switched them around until the amounts seemed right.

The policeman who came to the store told me it was the same thing as stealing. I got mad and cried when he said that, because it wasn't. I told him that my brothers did it all the time, and no one ever told them it was stealing. I know now that it's not the right thing to do, but I still hate going to Longs because I know about the security people watching from the tinted windows up above the pharmacy. Even though it was three years ago, I feel like they are still keeping an eye on me.

I go straight to the back of the store. Aisle Thirteen: Feminine Hygiene Products. The aisle I have avoided for months. I suppose most girls come down this aisle the first time with their moms, but that's not going to happen for me since I haven't even seen my mom since last fall. The first time I saw the spots of light blood in my underwear, I knew my whole life was changing. I sat on the bathroom floor for a long time, staring at the slate tiles and trying to figure things out. I didn't want anyone to know. While I was very good at keeping secrets, this kind of secret was complicated. I couldn't stop the blood from coming out.

I make a quick pass down the aisle full of pads, then loop back around. I turn my eyes sideways as I walk and catch the brand names on the boxes. The "growing up and liking it" lady in sixth grade suggested picking out whatever box design we liked best. I don't like any of the box designs. I take in the words quickly—Maxi, Mini, Mini-Maxi, Extra-Light Flow, Heavy Flow, Super Heavy. Okay, Super Heavy?

I reach sideways and pull down the medium-blue box, keeping my eyes straight ahead. Three other boxes somersault to the floor. I shove all four boxes back onto the metal shelf and walk toward the exit with my heart racing. I want to just leave but I can't. The sock between my legs is shifting; the inside of my thigh wet. I can smell it, the brown and ruby blood all mixed up.

I take my sweatshirt and tie it around my waist, just like the kindergarten teacher showed me when I forgot to put on underwear beneath my dress one morning. I know they are watching me now from the tinted windows upstairs. I am really being a freak in the store.

Then I come up with an idea. Why I didn't think of it earlier is beyond me. Aisle Seven: Office and School Supplies. I look for the yellow-orange school folders with sports drawings on the front and back, and the words "Pee-Chee—All-Season Portfolio" on the front. We use them all the time in school to keep papers in. There is a multiplication table on the inside cover. Nineteen cents each.

I pick up two and walk back to the aisle full of pads. I grab the medium-blue box and wedge it between the two Pee-Chee folders. My box of embarrassing pads is now covered on the front and the back, and I can walk to front of the store and pay for it. I keep my eyes down and set my supplies on the counter with the Pee-Chees carefully placed on top. I realize there will be a moment when the box of pads will be seen by everyone.

The store clerk picks up the two Pee-Chee folders and drops them into a paper bag. Then he picks up the box of pads and looks at it like he's confused. He turns the box around and around like he's trying to figure out what they are. He calls out loudly across the registers, "Bob, I need a price check on Stayfree maxi-pads."

I want to disappear forever. I didn't change any price tags.

My lip begins to quiver, and I bite down hard to make it stop. I hate Emily Fink. I hate "growing up and liking it."

"Three-fifty-nine!" shouts Bob.

I pull the folded bills from my pocket. My eyes stay glued to the smooth counter surface as I take the change in my hand. I walk through the swinging glass doors out of Longs with a bulky paper bag, my blood-stained jeans, and my two new Pee-Chee folders.

NOW

four-by-four photograph

An hour later, I peek back into the bathroom. The blood has been wiped clean from the floor. My mom is asleep. I tiptoe over to her, feeling a sudden strong desire to touch her. I stare at the shallow dish that has formed below her high, freckled cheekbone from her lack of eating. I could place a warm brown egg there and it would stay.

As she sleeps, my brilliant, reckless mother appears peaceful for the first time since I can remember. I wish I could stay here and study the lines and contours of her face for hours. What might I discover if I just slowed down and accepted her as she is now? I'm still searching for something here and I can't find it. I lean in closer to look at her.

Suddenly, she grabs my arm with what seems like a newborn's reflex, looks up at me, and opens her eyes wide—strange, like a fish coming up to the surface for a bubble of air. All the muscles and thin flesh of her face pull back so that I can see her eyes, the yellow whites and the deep blue staring up at me. She holds her gaze on me, almost like a Kabuki actor in the moment of their *mie*—the wide-eyed moment when the character's truth is finally revealed.

I try to read her. Is she saying, "Look at me" or "Take me in one last time" or "Help me"?

Her intense gaze sends a current, cold and startling, down into my throat. Then her eyes fall shut. I place my hand near her lips to feel for her breath against my palm.

I call out for my aunt.

"What? What's happening?" She races into the room.

My mom's throat begins to rattle like a carburetor.

"I–I don't know. She did something strange and I thought something was wrong."

My mother's breathing softens and she's back in a deep sleep.

"I think she's just tired again." My aunt sighs. It's clear that my mother's rally has faded. Now there is nothing to do except wait.

"I'll sit with her for a while," my aunt says.

I retreat upstairs to take a shower, longing for the water and steam to help me relax. But instead, the noise and pressure of the water heightens my emotional state. Everything swells inside me—and I am thankful for the falling water and the whirring fan overhead that mask my unbridled sobbing.

When I return to the bedroom, I gather her letters and attempt to put them in some kind of chronological order. I need to pull these pieces of my mother together into a complete portrait that I hope, in some strange way, will make me whole as well. I know that some of her letters were written before she left us—but others were written after she left and the divorce was still pending. And then she was suddenly traveling abroad and debating what her future might hold. Honestly, rather than a history, the letters are more like messages from bottles that have washed ashore from different continents.

I start at the beginning.

Dearest Gran,

I am in my usual state of disgrace with myself for having failed to get in touch with you. My friend Karen calls me from work yesterday and asks me to meet her for lunch. I come bipping up expecting to hear we have been fired, or worse, and she pounces on me with "We are both handing in our resignations on Wednesday and leaving for Europe in the beginning of October." I thought she was being facetious, but by golly, she isn't—and it is infectious. So infectious that I already have a ride to New York on the 15th of September! Karen will be going to St. Louis on the 19th with her brother who is—thank the Lord, pray the Lord—returning from Vietnam. She will then come back to New York, and we'll be off. We would be gone about two months and home in time for Christmas. So, Gran, you can see how I have had quite a bit on my mind as of late.

The children are all so beautiful and doing so well. Darling Melissa just had her third birthday, and I spent a ridiculous amount of time looking for her present. I gave her an Austrian music box, and she just delights in watching the little peasant girl on top spin around while it plays "Hi-Lili." The boys have learned how to swim—though Eden refuses to swim on top of the water. Both little fishes. Melissa is content to paddle around in her ring. Hopefully she will soon learn not to fear the water. She howls bloody murder anytime anyone splashes her— imperiously demands that they stop right away. A regular little queen she thinks she is—but still full of love and good humor.

*I will keep you abreast on the Europe plans—I only hope
I can manage finances. If I do manage to go, you will have
to think of something very special you want me to bring you.
Maybe a goat from the Swiss Alps?*

Now I realize that this was the trip that got postponed, or
"scotched" as my mother put it in her other letter to Gran.
Regardless, what was my dad thinking when she told him of her
plans to travel to Europe for two months? Maybe he believed she
would return from these travels restored and ready to come back
to the family. But it's clear she pulled further away instead.

In this next letter to my aunt, my mom is in the midst of her
travels.

Happy Halloween, my sister!

*At least I think today is the 31st. Oh, I am sad right now—
but rather deliriously sad. O my Redeemer, but your sister
has done a loon bit again. Now I am hopelessly gaga over a
Yugoslav boy who was a waiter on the ship we came down
from Rijeka on. Lucien Bugoni speaks little English. What
a giggle our conversations were. He'd probably bore me to
death if I could really talk to him. Poor me and my affinity for
young, blond non-sophisticates. Pas de quoi. I will love him
forever and ever!*

*Prior to meeting Bugoni, I was all decided to come back
home and attack J. without mercy 'til he agreed to remarry.
I'll have to return to that thought in a few days' time perhaps.
Karen has met a Yugoslav doctor who lives in Blato but*

vacations here three months of the year. I have not seen her in a while. Needless to say, we are not digging much culture right now.

Rijeka was awful. We were literally chased through the streets by a lunatic and ducked into a café for sanctuary only to find all men who couldn't speak or understand English or French, whereupon they threw a bottle of beer in my face and started a brawl. Fortunately the police returned our passports. Jane would faint dead to hear some of our adventures and circumstances. This is not a typical letter from a cultured young lady traveling abroad. So I am not particularly cultured—but a good letter may bore you.

It comes back to me now, the photographs of my mom on the boat with Lucien Bugoni. And the photos with her friend Karen. She told me about this trip to Europe when Bella, Dominic, and I came to visit her in Olympia several years ago. Bella sat next to me at the kitchen table drawing a fully clothed bunny. I asked my mom if I could look at some of her old photos, and she pulled out a tattered box full of loose pictures. Many of them I had never seen before.

In one photograph, my mom is strikingly beautiful. Her smile, as wide as I have ever seen it, caught in a frame of laughter. A white, tailored button-up shirt and a short tweed skirt. Sexy bent legs. There are wavy curls in her hair like she's paid special attention to it.

I lifted my eyes from the image. Here was my mom sitting across from me at her kitchen table, penciling in the Sunday crossword puzzle. Her eyes were slightly swollen and the color in her face a jaundiced yellow. She had aged radically in the past year (but that of course was before we knew about the cancer).

"Someday, I'm going to get all those photographs in a proper album," she said.

I looked back down at the image. It was an old-style color photo, four-by-four square with a white border. My mom in her tweed skirt, another woman in tall boots, and two men flanking them. All four are smiling for the camera, standing in front of an ocean and a postcard-blue sky.

I asked her about the photograph and who these people were. She came around behind me, picked up the photo, and held it at a distance. She paused and squinted at it as if she were flipping through pages in time, traveling back to that day in a matter of moments.

She told me the photograph was taken in Greece. "Corfu, to be exact."

She pointed to Karen, her roommate from San Francisco that she lived with for a brief time in Haight-Ashbury. She can't recall the names of the two men. "A couple of Greeks who offered to take us out to lunch," she said. "We were good-looking gals traveling alone. We got a lot of offers, and we usually accepted them."

She smiled and stepped away to refill her coffee mug. I looked over at Bella concentrating on the small buttons and details of the bunny's dress. She didn't like to miss a single detail.

I found more photos with the same bright sea, foreign men, and white borders. The handsome dark man with the chiseled jaw and thick cream-colored sweater seemed to be the favorite subject of my mom and her friend.

"What year was this?" I asked.

She paused again. "That was '69."

It's an easy calculation for me. I was four then.

"How long were you in Greece?" I asked, keeping my eyes on her smile in the photograph.

"Couple of months. But we didn't just go to Greece. We traveled all around Europe."

I didn't say anything else. I knew we were on completely different boats, and I couldn't bridge the ocean between us. She looked at the photo and recalled that youthful time of freedom. I looked at the photograph and thought, *I was four and I wanted a mother*. She was in Greece, smiling in a white, tailored button-up shirt and a short tweed skirt. Sexy legs. I kept staring at the photograph, drawn in by her youth and beauty. She is happy, undeniably so.

I imagined another photograph, one that might have been taken on that same day. One where my mom is home with us on the steps outside our San Jose duplex with the peach tree in the backyard. I can see my brothers and me next to her. They would be shirtless, and our lips would be stained by orange Popsicles—or maybe our faces would be dirty from the Carnation frozen chocolate malts that we ate off flat wooden spoons. Jamie, Eden, and I would be smiling.

But I can't see my mom's smile in that image. She wouldn't be smiling anything like the way she was smiling that day in Greece. She wouldn't have those soft curls in her hair. There's no way she would have been that happy.

At that moment, I reached my hand out to my daughter, Bella, and gently squeezed her forearm. It felt so warm against my palm. I smiled with closed lips, full of love for her. She looked up from her drawing and gave me the same smile back. Our smiles were neither wide nor full of Greek laughter, but we were fully present in that moment.

NOW

permanent ink

It's my mom's last birthday. She's made it to sixty-five. I wake up thinking that we should get her a cake with dark chocolate frosting and sixty-five striped candles. My aunt subtly reminds me that my mother doesn't have the strength to blow out candles. How stupid of me. My aunt shrugs and says, "The thought still counts."

My mom and I haven't spent many birthdays together. My aunt Janet, who was married to my father's brother, recently revealed to me that our grandmother Rita used to ask her to send gifts to our house on our birthdays and pretend our mother had sent them. My dad had to play along, even though this really bothered him. I do know for certain that the handmade doll from "Merry" was from my mom. I also know for certain that this is the last birthday my mom will have.

I sit on the upstairs bedroom floor holding a letter she wrote to me long ago and never sent. The paper is still bright yellow, as if it never saw much light over the years.

Melissa,

I have sharpened tomorrow's crossword pencil (already, because there are things I REALLY want to say to you...and it seems that there is very little opportunity). Let's accept that it's due to the ever-present "embarrassment"—a symbol of the distance that we have kept between us. Oh Kumquat! I do miss you so very much. Ever have I missed your girl-self—the contained but centralized you in a phantasmagorical childness. But now—oh baby-mine—I feel so deeply your destiny. Suddenly—to me, cuz we spend sporadic time together—you have so many facets. I want to explore them with you, darlin'. I have this enormous need for us to be honest with one another. I feel that we keep reaching for each other, ironically, tentative touches. Somehow we tend to back off...too often. I am unburdening myself as dawn pinkens. Memories, Sweet Pea, Loo-Lah, Liddy Bumpkins. And sorrow for all I forsook. There is no need to forsake more, however—at least I hope not.

Her ink is permanent. I feel her reaching out to me here—maybe overreaching with her whimsical language. ("Phantasmagorical" is a word I need to look up, for example.) But she liked to play with words that were colorful and elevated, and I love that piece of her.

May I please come back into your life a little more? Can we maybe help each other more often? I wrote you months ago and said I would be really direct and forward with you, but I have failed miserably at that. No more?? The next time one of us tries to get a bit inside the other and the "embarrassment" gets in the way, maybe we could wink or something—give a signal that it's okay, we're trying. I've been realizing how long it has been for you, recognizing me as the person I am as opposed to the figure I am supposed to represent. You sure are something, darlin'—you've hung in a long time. Perhaps a while longer?

It's clear she *was* yearning to be close with me...at least at some point or on some level. It seems like this should satisfy me, but there's a nagging question inside my head: Am I the one who's failed her? Was it me who was too afraid to let her in?

When I was in junior high, my dad pleaded with my mom to leave Washington and come live closer to us. He told her she needed to be "more goddamn involved" in her children's lives and that we could all benefit from having the guidance of another parent around. She wasn't committed to a job or a boyfriend at the time, so she acquiesced and drove down from Washington to California in her red Datsun.

I was ecstatic to help my mom find the little blue Victorian house by the railroad tracks downtown. Now she was a bicycle ride away. She got a job serving cocktails at the local bar, the Bit-a-Honey, and quickly hooked up with one of the regular customers. Things seemed okay for a while.

Until she came into my room late one night.

THEN

gone

I am underneath my Indian wool blanket. Sleeping. Dreaming, perhaps. My bedroom door opens and light from the hallway floods in. Her shadow approaches my bed and she sits heavily. I can smell her, my mother: smoke-drenched dungarees, red wine, Ysatis, and Amaretti di Saronno. She sits next to me and I don't feel like waking up. I hate these late night wake-ups. It's always something that could wait for morning.

"Darlin'? Darlin', I need to go," she mumbles.

Her hands are cool and damp on my shoulder. She's not looking at me—just talking with her head drawn down, almost like she's talking to herself. Her voice is soft and garbled.

"I can't stay, darlin'. I just can't. I'd stay if I could, but I hate California, everything about it. There are too many people here, too many cars driving on the road. You can't understand how I hate it."

I shift my body under the covers. "What time is it, Mom?"

"It's late, darlin'. Three a.m. or something."

"Where are you going?"

"I'm going back to Washington. I'm better there. My friends are there."

She fidgets with a set of jingly keys on her lap. "I'm sorry to wake you. I just wanted you to know."

"It's okay, Mom. Maybe you'll feel better in the morning. We can get doughnuts."

"No. I'm going to drive back tonight. I should make it as far as Eureka."

I can see the edges of the taped-up cards and horse pictures on my bedroom walls behind her head. The ones I put up before she came back. The ones that were supposed to make her stay. She leans in and kisses my cheek. Her face is wet, her breath heavy with liquor.

"I'm so sorry, darlin'. I'll send you a letter soon."

"It's okay, Mom," I repeat. It's all I know how to say.

She stands slowly and walks out into the yellow halo of light coming through the doorway.

Somewhere inside me I have a voice that can scream out to her, *Please don't go, Mom. You can't leave again.* But instead, once again, I give her permission with the only words I can find—"It's okay, Mom."

I don't even take my head off the pillow. I just watch her leave. I hear every sound: the front door opening, then clicking shut; her uneven footsteps descending the stairs; the creaking of her car door opening, then slamming with a finality. *Maybe not every girl needs a mother,* I say to myself.

I hear the engine rev and the wheels roll out of the driveway. I pull myself into a tight ball. I don't feel anything, not even the sheets against my skin. I am nowhere, with no one touching me, and she is gone.

NOW

ache

Back upstairs, I reach for a letter scripted on white butcher paper that I figure must have been written sometime after she fled back to Washington.

Dear Melissa,

It is agony without you. Your wonderful letter filled me with equal amounts of longing, pride, and loving. What a kid! And with so little time left to be a kid. Especially when your very own mother compels you to deal with situations as disturbing as ours. I am very proud of you. You seem to be meeting the fact of our being apart with great strength. I just pray that in overcoming the pain you have not had to close off your emotional self— that you are keeping in touch with your soul. May it never be too painful for you to look inside and to share all that you find within. There is so much beauty in you that it would be selfish to lock it away. And beauty includes any pain or anger—all things must have balance.

I sit down on the hardwood floor to take in these beautiful, yearning words of hers. Here are her sincere wishes for me to find my voice. And I'm touched that she understands this piece of me that locks emotions away. She must have been sensing how difficult things were going to get for me heading into adolescence. Around this time, things did begin to unravel and lose their "balance." My mom was back in Washington working as a cocktail waitress when I began to notice boys. She might have warned me about the trouble that was coming, and how awful kissing a boy could be.

THEN

first dance

W hen Charlie Ross came up to me at school and asked if I would go to the seventh-grade dance with him, I didn't even know who he was. I looked at him and felt my stomach do a flip turn. I shot my eyes both ways down the row of blue lockers to see if anyone was listening, or worse, playing some kind of joke. He asked again. Finally I mustered up, "I don't know," and walked away, pressing my school binder against my chest. I should have said no.

"Are you crazy, Melissa?" my friend Lola said when I told her. "He is cute. You have to say yes."

"Cute" had not crossed my mind. He had a shark tooth dangling from a thin, gold chain around his neck. He was skinny and pale. Feathered black hair, small dark eyes, and a mouth that seemed a size too big for his face. The way he stood in front of me with his chest pushed out made me think of our cocky rooster, Russell Sage, the one that bosses all the hens around in the pasture. I was more afraid than intrigued.

"You know he's sort of popular. I'm going to say yes for you," Lola told me.

I wanted to fit in. I agreed because she said she would do the talking for me, and because I don't have any other friends like Lola—straight-A smart, funny, and confident talking to boys she hardly knows. Lola is pretty, but not stuck-up pretty. She wears glasses that magnify her dark chocolate eyes to the size of Junior Mints. Her hair is thick and shiny in a perfect Dorothy Hamill flip.

Lola is the one who told me that I needed to buy Sticky Fingers jeans as soon as possible. She always dresses in tight jeans and stretchy shirts that show off the fact that she has breasts. I do the opposite; I wear loose-fitting shirts because I don't have anything to show.

Lola also likes to talk about her Greek name. If a boy asks her name, she tells them the whole name, Lolita Constance Kalliope. I decide to go to the dance in hopes that some of her confidence will rub off on me. I decide to go because maybe Dylan Peters, the boy who smiled at me from across the gym, will be there.

But once I'm there, nothing is as I imagined it would be. Charlie Ross has edged me to the corner of the gym. He is holding me and pressing his skinny, flat chest against mine. He pushes his oversized lips against mine and sticks his tongue in my mouth—far into my mouth. I try to turn my head away, but he holds me firmly as he shoves his tongue back in. His tongue is doing a fast, gyrating dance all around inside my mouth. Orange and pink lights spin in circles on the floor. I don't recognize the music. I have never been kissed before…and it's *horrible*.

When the music slows down, he is like a huge dog on top of me, sweating and slobbering into my mouth. This cannot be normal. He pumps out what feels like a steady stream of warm sink water into my mouth. I cannot possibly swallow it. I push my lips against my shoulder and let it seep out into the sleeve of my gauze shirt. It's all I can do to keep from gagging before he shoves his tongue back in. I soak my sleeve over and over and wait for the lights to change, the music to stop.

Kissing, I thought, would be delicate. I thought it would taste like honeysuckle flowers. Who knew it involved this tongue business? I thought I would pause and smile between the kisses like they do on *The Love Boat* every Friday night.

I finally extract myself and shout over the music, "I need to get something to drink."

Charlie Ross pulls me hard against him, and I feel how much stronger he is than me. I am the chicken girl. I am the small end of the wishbone after it snaps in two.

"Okay and then we come right back here," he says.

I rush over to the lighted classroom that has been set up for drinks and snacks. Lola is sitting down with a Coke and the boy she came with. A couple of other kids are sitting with them. They are doing what Lola said we would be doing—hanging out and talking. I give Lola a "please rescue me" look, but she doesn't get it. She gives me a discreet thumbs-up. This is her idea of the road to popularity. She will tell me that making out with a boy at a dance puts me in a whole new category of popularity.

"What do you want?" Charlie Ross asks me.

I can hardly look at him in his tight, black disco pants. Instead I look at the array of candy and soda, and I want it all—Kit Kats, Butterfingers, Ding Dongs, Life Savers, Red Vines, Juicy Fruit gum, and Hostess CupCakes. I want to do nothing more than sit in this classroom and stuff myself with every kind of candy and soda imaginable.

"What do you want?" he asks me again.

I pick up the Hostess orange cream cupcakes with the white curlicues across the top.

"And Fresca," I say.

I walk over to Lola and give her another look. I notice for the first time that she is wearing makeup—a smudge of blue powder across her eyelids. She whispers in my ear, "You are so lucky, Melissa."

She has no idea.

I eat the cupcakes as slowly as I possibly can to stall going back to the dance floor. I peel off the flat layer of frosting and take tiny bites into the white curlicues. As thirsty as I am, I measure each sip. Charlie Ross stands up. He fidgets with his empty soda can.

"Come on. Let's go," he says.

I cannot go back into the strobe lights where I don't know how to say no and he will shove himself against me and stick his tongue into my mouth.

Dylan Peters, with his waves of sun-bleached hair, walks into the room and stands in front of Charlie.

"Hey, dude," he says with a nod. I stop eating. Dylan Peters glances at me and smirks. I have no idea what that means, but it is very different from the way he smiled at me across the gymnasium. It seems like a look of disappointment—like I'm one of those loose girls. Maybe he smiled at me before because he could tell I had yet to be kissed. Sick to my stomach, that's how I feel when Dylan Peters smirks at me.

At least now we are doing what Lola promised, hanging out together and talking in a group.

Charlie says, "Let's go," for the third time.

Lola squints her big eyes at me all of a sudden. "Melissa, do you have something in your shirt pockets?"

"No. What are you talking about?" I say. But I know exactly what she is talking about.

"It just looks like you have something in your pockets."

"No," I say again, wishing I had my school binder to shove up against my chest. On a school day, I can cover the fact that I'm flat chested.

But I know exactly what Lola is seeing. Before the dance I folded thick squares of toilet paper into the two front pockets of my white gauze shirt. I was very careful to smooth each square out and measure it exactly. I picked the shirt out of my drawer because I saw its potential. I saw that the two front pockets were perfectly placed over where I had small budding lumps. If I could just pad the pockets a little, I thought it would make me appear more like a girl should at a seventh-grade dance.

Lola looks genuinely confused, but she's drawing too much attention to me. I turn my body away from the group.

"I'm going to the bathroom," I say.

Charlie Ross lets out an obvious sigh.

In the girls' bathroom, I stand in front of the long mirror and look at the pockets on my shirt. The light at home was much different, not like the bright fluorescent glare of school lights. Now I can see the pockets are a different shade of white from the rest of the shirt and just how stupid it looks. Now what do I do? Take out the tissue or leave it? I'm busted either way. In the bathroom stall, I take out half of the tissue and leave the rest in case Lola asks me how come my pockets look so different all of a sudden.

I run my fingertips along the rows of blue lockers as I wander back to the gymnasium. I think of ways to act, directions to run. I don't want to be attending dances or kissing boys. I want to be home in my room or up on the hay bales in the barn so I can think for a long time about everything that's happening.

I don't know which is the worse place to be now—under the lights where I am on display as the flat-chested girl who has stuffed her pockets with toilet paper, or in the dark corner where Charlie Ross will shove his tongue in my mouth. Someday I am going to clear all the gravel out of my throat. I am going to have a voice. I will be brave and I will say no.

But right now, I am going back to the queasy corner of the dance floor with Charlie Ross. I will spit into my sleeve and count the seconds until it is over. I will have Lola tell him at school on Monday that I have a boyfriend at another school. It is the only lie I can think of as Charlie Ross's tongue slips back into my mouth.

NOW

a handful of butterflies

When I touch my mother's forearm at her bedside, it is damp with sweat. I want her to wake up. But she is in another world. My mom's husband, Kim, takes up the space next to her on the bed. He clicks the channel changer from station to station. The little dogs are tucked tightly against her body. I don't belong in the room right now.

I walk out to the living room and sink into the blue chair that once lived in our yellow house. It is worn and the springs underneath are shot. This blue chair belonged to Grandma Rita and came to us after she died. Many years later I learned that she had frozen to death in her own backyard.

"She had been drinking and slipped on the ice," my dad tearfully told me one night. "There was no one there to help her back up."

My father and his brothers flew to New York to divide up her belongings. When he returned, new pieces of furniture and antiques appeared throughout the rooms of our yellow house. For the first time, we had a cabinet filled with beautiful dishes, sterling silver spoons, and colorful glass objects. Finally, a feminine presence I had been longing for crept into the house and I felt connected to my grandmother through those lovely, tangible things in the china cabinet.

I'm thankful now for the comfort and familiarity of the blue chair's thick down cushions. The memories sewn into this chair are part of who I am and where I come from. This is the chair my grandmother held her babies in. This is the chair where she drank martinis to soothe her sorrows after her six-week-old baby boy died. This is the chair that landed upstairs in my dad's attic room for many years. It sat across from a small wood-burning stove and comforted many a drunk and stoned visitor.

This is the chair that I slept on when no one was home. The chair that I rescued from our yellow house. It traveled with me to a basement apartment in San Francisco. It slept in a Santa Rosa barn until I knew where I was going next. This is the chair that eventually moved to Los Angeles with me while I was in college. The chair I sat in while pregnant with my son. The chair that was too heavy to move to Boston and lived in a dark storage facility for two years. The chair I sat in and nursed my daughter. The chair my husband said was "ratty and falling apart." He insisted that it was aggravating his allergies and that we needed to get rid of it.

Years ago, we helped my mom lift the chair into the back of her van, and she drove it here to her house in Olympia. Now it is covered with white dog hair and its upholstery is threadbare. But even with its broken springs, this chair is still the most comfortable chair in the whole world. This blue chair that now holds me in the house where my mom will die.

I feel my grandmother Rita's gaze on me. Or is it her hand

resting on mine? I think about her butterfly collection that I tried to fix when I was ten. My dad brought it into my room one afternoon along with a handful of other treasures. There were dozens of butterflies in the collection, all crowded into a boxy acrylic frame. Their wings were attached to paper bodies in shades of pale green and yellow. The butterflies had shifted and migrated to one side of the frame. I could tell that the box had been improperly stored or shipped sideways. I tried to shift the butterflies back to the center of the frame with no luck. And so I pulled off the acrylic face of the box. This was my first mistake.

I laid out each butterfly on my bed. They were bright blue, lavender, and yellow; spotted, speckled, tangerine, and iridescent. Some had wings with visible veins like tiny rivers on an antique map. One had wings the color of Indian curry with inky black edges.

The butterflies were difficult to pick up, and the glue holding the paper bodies against their wings had turned brittle. I held a lemon-yellow and black butterfly between my fingers and studied it, unaware that my fingerprints would rub its colorful dust away. I set my favorite, a magnificent blue-and-black butterfly, in front of me. It shimmered like my mother's blue eye shadow and black lashes.

I attempted to fix the butterflies and put them back into the box in some kind of rational order. But the more I handled them, the more damaged they became. I set aside several with tattered wings and detached bodies. I wished then that I had just let them be.

I wanted to know my grandmother—and by loving her

treasures, I thought I could at least connect with her sensibilities. I needed to take care of the things she had left behind.

Eventually, I lost my grandmother's collection of butterflies. I can't recall where or when they got lost but they are gone, along with most everything I ever had of hers. Over time, the pieces of my grandmother have been lost, stolen, and sold. I wonder if it will be like this with my mom too. What will I hang on to—to remember her?

I pull my knees up to my chest, close my eyes, and sink deeper into the blue chair. There was so much that happened inside and outside of our yellow house that she wasn't aware of. So much she missed.

THEN

pennies on the dashboard

We make a lot of trips down Center Road to the 7-Eleven. This morning my dad asks me to come with him to pick up some breakfast cereal before school. I'm in eighth grade. When my dad is upset or nervous about something, he says "Jesus Christ" a lot, and I mean a *lot*. He has already said it five times and we are not even to 7-Eleven yet.

"What's wrong, Dad?"

He is silent for a few moments.

"I'm in a bad situation. *A really bad situation*," he says.

We pull into the 7-Eleven parking lot. "Jesus," he says for the sixth time.

"What's so bad about it?" I ask.

"You see that change?" He points his finger to the console between the two seats in the van—we call it the dashboard. I look down. I see Dentyne gum wrappers, Tic Tacs, a tipped can of Pepsi, and an empty bottle of Excedrin. There are coins too. A handful of pennies, some dimes and quarters. It's exactly how the dashboard usually looks.

"That's it," he says. "That is *all* we have."

My dad can be a real joker, a teller of tall tales.

"What do you mean?" I ask.

"That change there is the only money I have to my name right now."

I don't believe him until I see that his eyes are full of water, like he might cry. I can tell by the way his hands are squeezing the top of the steering wheel. It's not the first time he's told me about the money problem, but he's never said that it was down to the change on the dashboard.

"I'll tell you this though, Melissa. I am going to figure it out. I don't know how yet, but I am not going to let you kids down."

I believe what he says but I am also scared.

"You wait in the van. I'll be right out," he says.

He starts scooping the coins into his hands. He leaves behind the pennies that are sticky with Pepsi. I watch him walk into the 7-Eleven to buy cereal.

Now I feel awful for stealing the forty-nine cents off his dresser. I've done it at least four times because that's how much four-inch houseplants cost at Goodman Building Supply. Just last week I pedaled down there on my ten-speed. I know every variety of plant they sell at Goodman's: rabbit-foot ferns, emerald ripples, creeping Charlies, spider plants, and piggybacks. Just forty-nine cents for a living plant. At the time, it seemed like such a good price.

My dad is quiet when he gets back into the van. He doesn't say "Jesus Christ" or talk about money as we drive.

"Don't worry, Dad," I say. "You're right. It's all going to work out."

He doesn't respond.

There must be something that I can do to help him. One by one, I start to unstick the pennies from the dashboard and stack them in piles of ten. Short stacks of sticky copper pancakes. As if that's going to save us.

THEN

the devil under jamie's bed

From the hallway, I can hear Jamie swearing in his room.
"Goddamn motherfucker," he says.

It is early on a Friday morning before school. I pull on a pair of white tube socks and walk quietly into his room. He is sitting up, tanned and bare chested in a tangle of wool blankets. He swears all the time lately.

"That fuckin' thing was here last night," he says to me. His eyes are slightly swollen and deep pink around the edges. I don't need to say, "What *thing?*" I know what he's talking about, and I know things are happening in our yellow house these days that cannot be explained.

He first told me about it, this thing, a few months ago. It hasn't left my mind, the way his hands were shaking and his eyes were wide and different that morning.

"It's a little dark motherfucker devil that hides under my bed when I go to sleep." He said it wakes him in the middle of the night by shaking his bed from underneath. He said he's scared shitless, but he can't get out of the bed because it's shaking so badly.

"This ain't my fucking imagination," he reminds me. He told

me he's actually *seen* it twice. Sometimes it will dart out from underneath his bed and hide in the corners and the shadows of the room—a small animallike creature, always silent and afraid of the light. Whatever it is, he claims it to be part devil or something the devil sent. He said it follows him everywhere, even when he was up in Washington visiting Mom, even when he spent the night at Matt Pheffer's house. I know my brother, and he might be a liar sometimes, but he does not make up stories. Eden makes up stories, but not Jamie.

"Dad thinks it's a bunch of bullshit," says Jamie, kicking the striped blanket onto the floor. I sit on the end of his mattress because I can tell he needs someone to believe him. I'm trying to come up with an answer, but I don't really have one. Ever since he started high school and wearing Ben Davis pants, we don't talk much. Part of me is glad just to be sitting here with him when he's not bragging about how tough he is.

Right now, I see my brother who loves to fish for steelhead, read *Field and Stream* magazines from cover to cover, and draw amazing pictures. He says he's going to drop out of school, get out of this crappy town, join the marines, and cover himself in tattoos. My dad says if Jamie is not going to finish high school, then he can't live in our house.

"Look what it did last night," Jamie says. He points to the giant oak headboard behind him. I see it then, a two-inch-wide crack in the wood. It's a vertical split from the top, about a foot long.

"How did that…" I pause. "When did that happen?" I ask.

"It split the bed in two, in case you can't see that," he says. "Sounded like a fucking lightning bolt hit me in the head."

I lean all the way forward and stick my finger into the fresh split in the wood. This is not a lightweight bed; this is a bed that has been around for a hundred years. It is solid and sturdy with fat acorns hand-carved into its thick edges. *Man, Dad is going to be pissed off*, I think to myself. I am bothered by something as I pull my finger out of the splintered oak—the split goes down against the grain of the wood. I know from wood-shop class that wood gets split along the grain. That is the way people cut wood and that's the way wood works. My mouth turns dry, like I have swallowed every bit of spit in my mouth. Jamie did not do this—he is not a bed splitter.

The little devil creature jumps into my world right then, because it is not just in Jamie's head anymore. I see what it is capable of. I slide off the broken bed and head toward the door. I don't want to think about this right now. I don't want to be this afraid. I want to go back to my room where all my knickknacks and glass animals are in order. I need them in order. I need the blue glass birds next to the nest of blue marbles. I need the tiny elephant beads to stay hidden inside the metal box.

We're all changing so fast. I don't know what to believe anymore. My dad really doesn't understand what's going on when he's not around. He doesn't know that I am stealing change off the top of his dresser, that Jamie is drunk and stoned too much, and that Eden is experimenting with drugs. We are all heading in the wrong direction. I look back at Jamie. He's scared. I walk out of the room, glad that it is day, glad that there is light.

NOW

mind and heart

I sit at the upstairs desk, deciphering every sound in the house. The paws of dogs padding across the hardwood floors, the television downstairs tuned to a sports channel, my aunt turning the pages of her book and sighing in the room across from me. This last birthday of my mom's feels completely uncelebrated. How can I leave Olympia with all of these unsettled pieces still rattling around inside me?

There are things of my mom's that I would like to take home with me. I grab the framed black-and-white photograph off the dresser and pack it in my suitcase. It's an old shot of my mom and Jamie that ran in the local newspaper, both of them young and beaming with huge, happy smiles. I will send it to Jamie when she dies so that he can remember how radiant her smile was then.

Again, I go back to my mother's folder of letters and dabbles. I pull out a letter to Jamie—never sent.

Jamie (Numero Uno),

Soon to be another year since you struggled into this world. How sad I am that you are struggling yet. I implore you, would that I could even bribe you—turn it over, my son. Please turn it over. I have been thinking of you so much these past weeks. It was no surprise to hear you were in jail—some sense of despair kept ragging at me. And though you are out now, the despair remains and I am truly frightened. It is as if I feel your despair, your loneliness, and your fear. You need to get help for your addiction and realize that you have been living in a world of demons and horrors that only exists in your mind and heart. You can deny it all you want—it is only part of the dream. Feeling the world is totally fucked, that the bomb could fall any day, that value is fleeting and therefore unimportant beyond the moment, some are born to suffer—all dream-stuff. Truth is you could have 50 years of gratification ahead of you—of embracing this life and yourself, and going for all you're worth, which is everything. It's time. I know. The message grows within me as strongly as you yourself once did. The hourglass is running out— acceleration as the sands dwindle—you cannot stay there any longer. Please come in. I am so afraid. I send my guardians to watch over you. Lord, I must sound nuts—but I am so afraid.

If only it weren't so late by then, Mom. You could have helped Jamie when he was struggling to find himself. This wasn't the first time he was in jail. I lost count of the times Jamie and Eden ended up in juvenile hall. Later, it was county jail. Drugs, vandalism, stupidity—I'm not sure what their records show. What stopped you, Mom, from sending your letters to us? Or from just coming back and hugging us?

THEN

african tomatoes

Our garden this year is abundant with huge, juicy beefsteak tomatoes, dark green and red chards, pole beans, curly lettuces, and cornstalks as tall as you'd find in Iowa. There are lemon cucumbers that we eat right off the vine like crunchy apples. There are giant zucchini and baby pink radishes. We are also the only family to have an African tomato tree growing in our garden.

My dad says that it's an extremely rare species of plant. I ask him when it will get its tomatoes, and he said it all depends on the number of full moons and certain weather patterns, and that we might have to wait some time before we see any fruit.

I've been keeping an eye on the African tomato plant, checking for signs of delicate yellow blossoms that could yield such rare fruit.

After school while I am taping up cards and pictures on the walls of my room, I hear my brothers rushing up from the bottom of the stairs. Both of them bound through my door out of breath, their faces flushed red. The entire African tomato tree is in their arms. Jamie has the front end and Eden holds the back end, dirty roots and all.

"What are you doing?" I scream.

"You gotta help us, Melissa," says Jamie.

"What did you do to our African tomato tree?"

Jamie laughs. "It's not an African tomato, Sis. There's no such thing."

I'm confused.

"It's dad's pot tree," says Eden.

I feel so stupid. "Just get *out* of my room!" I yell. I fully believed in that African tomato tree.

"No, no, we need to hide it in your closet, just 'til tomorrow."

"Come on, Melissa. We really need your help," says Eden.

"No. Go hide it in your own closet," I tell him.

"Your room is the only safe place. Besides, you're a lot cooler than you used to be, now that you're in junior high," says Jamie.

I can tell he's trying to soften me up, but I think about how it's true, that once you're in junior high, you have to act differently. Suddenly, my organized little room looks pathetic with everything in its place, and I think, yeah, I want to help them. I want to be a part of their club, whatever it is. I'm looking at both my brothers' flushed faces and their blue eyes against the vibrant green tree now standing upright in my room, and I see that I have a chance to be on the same side as them. Maybe I'm tired of doing everything right.

"Okay," I say.

Jamie turns the tree upside down and stuffs it up high into my closet, just like the Grinch does when he pushes little Cindy Lou Who's Christmas tree up the chimney.

"Hey, Jamie, take it easy on those leaves!" says Eden.

Then Eden sits on my bed and talks to me in a voice so nice that I feel like I can forgive him for that long-ago bloody nose. He pulls off a green leaf that is almost as big and broad as his hand.

"We're going to get frickin' rich off this stuff. You understand, Melissa? You see this one leaf? Each leaf is worth twenty-five to fifty cents. Now, look up there at all those thousands and thousands of leaves."

Jamie, Eden, and I stare up in the same way we used to when we stayed up late in our sleeping bags outside, searching for the Big and Little Dippers and shooting stars.

"And it's not even the leaves that are so valuable, it's the buds. Man, the buds are big money. Isn't that right, Jamie?"

Jamie nods like the expert. "You gotta keep your door shut between now and tomorrow because Dad has a nose for it."

"Well, what happens tomorrow?" I ask.

"Tomorrow after school, we bake it in the oven," says Jamie.

"But what happens when Dad finds out it's missing from the garden?"

Eden changes his tone. "Hey, you can't think about Dad in this. He shouldn't be growing this shit anyway. We're probably saving him from getting arrested. Right, Jamie?"

"Yeah, he's going to think one of his hippie friends ripped him off," Jamie says, laughing.

"Melissa, you better not mess up, or else someone is going to end up in jail," says Eden. "You get it. Right?"

"Yeah, I get it."

Once it turns dark, I tell my dad that I am tired and going to sleep a little early. But I am not tired at all. I am staring at the dark pine knots on my bedroom walls and thinking about the importance of my role. I am the keeper of the pot, the good one, the trusted one. But why can't I become something more? I could make money so I don't have to steal change from my dad's dresser anymore. I could become a dealer.

Overnight, I could quickly carve out a new image of myself at school. Instead of the quiet, flat-chested girl with the long, blond hair, I could be the girl with the long, blond hair who has pot for sale. I know people outside my brothers' circle that I could approach. Lola would definitely help me, and she said she would do anything to get popular. I might even be allowed on the field at lunch with the stoners if they knew I had something to offer. I could follow in my brothers' footsteps. I wouldn't have to smoke it, just sell it or at least be known for selling it.

My alarm clock goes off at four in the morning. I hit the snooze button and wait in bed, listening for sounds of anyone awake in the house. My room is quiet and completely dark. I crack the door open for some hallway light. I follow the thin line of light to the closet and reach my arms through clothes and jangly metal hangers until I feel the leafy branches. The delicate leaves are like feathers against my wrists, but the scent is staunch and crisp. It is a fresh smell, like the garden, but distinctly differ- ent from pole beans and lemon cucumbers.

My body rattles like the metal hangers as I pinch off my first leaf. The leaf is like my hand with five thin, reaching fingers. I pinch off another, and another. I count eight leaves. No one will notice just eight missing. Maybe I can take more. I think maybe fifteen. I am careful to pull each leaf from a different stem. I hold my fifteen leaves gently, like butterflies cupped in my hands, then set them behind my dresser so it looks as if a clump may have fallen there accidentally.

I lie back down on my bed, stiff and straight with my knees locked and a wild stirring still inside me. I reach my hands up underneath my shirt, feeling for the beginnings of breasts. Not much there, but they are small and soft like apricot halves, and I keep feeling them anyway. I am interesting and more alive than ever. Jamie and Eden were right. No one will ever suspect me, the good one, the one who always stays away from trouble. Now I have my own secret. I am full of mystery and potential, and I am on my way.

THEN

strip-searched

My mom is sitting at one of the booths at Happy Donuts with her hands wrapped around a cup of coffee. She's wearing her most elegant scarf—powder-blue silk with bright purple morning glories along the borders. Her sister sent it from New York. I wave hello to her, and she waves to the waitress to refill her coffee cup.

"The cinnamon rolls are sinfully good," she says as I slide into the booth across from her.

"Okay," I say. I quickly run my fingers along the underside of the table between us. An old habit.

"Sorry I haven't been around since I arrived."

"It's all right. I had a huge history test this week. Ninth grade is really hard."

"You heard what happened?"

"Sorta. I heard you got arrested."

The waitress sets a big spiral sweet roll in front of me and fills my mom's coffee cup.

"Yeah, I've never been so humiliated in my life," she says as she rips open two packets of sugar at the same time.

I pull at the edge of the sticky roll, thinking about when she arrived from Washington several nights ago. I knew she was drunk when she left our house. Her keys were dangling out of her back pocket, and she said that she was going to spend the night in Santa Rosa with her friends. She was wearing blue mascara.

"I'll stop by tomorrow night," she said as she sashayed out the door.

And I remember being annoyed with her because she was acting so happy about everything. I wondered why she couldn't at least spend more than two hours with us after driving all the way down from Washington. But I needed to study for history anyway, and I know better than to tell adults that they can't drive when they're drunk, because they can and they do.

"What did they actually pull you over for?" I ask, because I'm not stupid. I know that cops can't pull someone over unless they have a reason to. When Uncle Rich got arrested for drunk driving with my brothers and me in the backseat, the cop told him that swerving against the curb with three kids in the car was reason enough.

"They didn't pull me over. I flagged them down," says my mom.

"You *what?*"

"Well, I was lost, and I wanted to ask them where I was."

I can *so* see her doing this, batting her blue eyelashes and believing she was being charming by saying she was lost.

"Then they found the hunk of hash in my pocket, and everything went downhill from there."

My mom reaches over and snatches the center curl of my sweet roll, the part I was saving for last. "Just too tempting," she says, stuffing it into her mouth. And in the next second, the waitress rushes by and grabs my empty plate.

I stare at my mother in disbelief. She shrugs. "Get another one, if you want."

"That's all right," I say, looking at the table across from us. A lady with a plastic rain bonnet is holding a doughnut up with two hands and nibbling at it like a squirrel. I listen to the dips and rises of my mom's voice.

"You know, I brought that hash down for Ali's mom to help her through her chemo treatments."

I know this part is true. My friend Alison's mom has been sick for a long time. She's lost all of her thick, black hair. *How could my mom be so stupid and careless as to "flag down" the police?* If she had been smoking that hash as well, she would have put on that awful southern drawl she falls into when she smokes pot. My mom's transformation when she does drugs is something altogether unpredictable. She's tried to be cool with me before, and on several occasions she has leaned over me with a joint pinched between her fingers and casually asked, "You wanna a hit?" I was eleven the first time she asked.

"The worst part was that those goddamn Santa Rosa cops strip-searched me like a couple of dogs. Checked every inch of my body inside and out, if you catch my drift. I think they were getting off on it."

I turn my head around hoping that no one is paying attention. Novato is a small town. Happy Donuts is half the size of a single bowling lane.

"That's terrible, Mom," I say, keeping it low, wanting another cinnamon roll to pull apart. I avoid the deep well of her blue eyes. Instead I watch her strong hands, her fingers full of turquoise and silver. The single gold-and-garnet snake ring that is coiled around her ring finger. I hear her words as if they are far away and disjointed, like a radio with poor reception. The jail cell was cold. The cops were cruel. They didn't believe her story about why she had the hash.

I slide my hands back underneath the table and rub my fingertips along the surface, searching for lumps of old chewing gum. My brothers and I always used to count how many pieces we could find with our fingers as soon as we sat down at a truck-stop diner or a restaurant. We liked the feel of hardened gum and always added our own gum to the collection. It reminded us that there were other kids like us.

My mom lights up a Camel. I know she's making an effort, trying to share her thoughts and be candid with me. But I don't want this. These aren't the conversations I want to have with my mom. I want to tell her that things in the yellow house are starting to spin in all the wrong directions. I want to ask her if she has ever felt so scared of the world that she couldn't close her eyes at night. I want to ask her if she is going to spend the night on this visit. But I don't. Because I know better now than to ask the questions that have unpredictable answers.

I take in the edge of the vibrant morning-glory scarf along her neckline, wishing I could feel a small bit of the silk between my fingertips. I take in her breath of sugared coffee, cream, and unfiltered Camels. The diamond eye on her snake ring winks when the light hits it in just the right way. I funnel these small things into myself because that is all I can do for now.

What good would it do me to unravel the anger inside me?

I might hurl this heavy ceramic coffee cup across the table. I might stand up and tell her she sucks at being a mom. But that isn't me. I'll need to take her as she is right here, right now—fragrant, strip-searched, and full of mystery.

NOW

monsters

B ella calls to ask me if I have seen her stuffed cat Snowflake.
"Yes, I have Snowflake with me. Remember? You packed
her in my suitcase—to keep me company."

"Oh, I forgot." I don't think Bella forgot. I think she wants
to make sure I'm not neglecting Snowflake. Bella always packs
mementos or animals into my husband's suitcase when he travels.
Pure sweetness, this girl.

Bella used to call out for me in the middle of the night. "Mama,
stay with me," she'd cry. I'd stagger into her room and try to talk
her into sleeping on her own, but I never had a very good argument. So I'd lie by her side or scoop her up in my arms and take her
to our big bed. She's teaching me how to be a mother. Someday I
will tell her that she saved me, and she will probably roll her eyes.

"Make sure you bring Snowflake back," she says. "And Daddy
says to tell you that Uncle Eden called."

"Okay, but he knows I'm here with Mom, doesn't he?"

I'm concerned about Eden too but in a different way than Jamie.
He has funneled far too many drugs into his body over the years.
He's told me stories about "the people messing with him"—the

FBI, the CIA, and the Vietnamese Mafia. And then there are the people who supposedly have been changing the labels on his clothes while he sleeps and the gravestones that he thinks our father is illegally importing from eastern Europe.

Over the years, I've found myself memorizing the bizarre things Eden says in our brief and erratic conversations: "I'm like a chicken with a missing feather and they're coming after me, picking off all my loose feathers. I am in danger. There are mutant creatures living in my storage shed. I'm wearing eight-hundred-dollar fuckin' pants. I'm smoking crack and chasing it with Jim Beam and liquid Ativan. How many dead bodies have you seen in your life, Melissa? Man, I've been shooting for the stars all my life. I just need someone to believe in me. That's all I need. I've got nine thousand dollars stashed overseas and an ace of spades up my sleeve."

Right now, he's trying to get clean and his mind is more lucid each time I see him. But the road has been dangerous for Eden. He's been fighting his monsters and addictions for a long time now.

THEN

brick fight

The yelling comes from the brick patio outside my bedroom window. It's a fight. I wish I could tune it out, turn up the radio, but I always watch. I always listen.

I hear Eden yelling first. He comes into view in front of my window with its twelve separate square panes. My dad rushes behind him and grabs the back of Eden's AC/DC T-shirt. My dad's face is angry and red like the bricks. Eden's face is tight and white.

"Fuck you!" Eden screams and pushes my dad's arm out of the way. There is another push and another shove. I watch their bodies—my father, short and athletic, with runner's legs; my brother, lean and pale, with his gangly legs in a pair of corduroy bell-bottoms. I watch their bodies hit the ground as they roll across the bricks like two kids pretending to be wrestlers.

Then I don't hear any sound. It's like the drive-in movies without the volume—the times when our live-in had us sit outside the car without the speakers so she could make out with her boyfriend in the front seat.

Eden has his hand around my dad's throat. I don't think my dad can breathe.

I always watch them fight, but usually stay well out of the way. But this time I scream.

"Please stop!" I scream. But no one hears me inside my room.

My dad throws Eden off him. Eden spits at him, scrambles, and runs down the hill toward the long driveway that leads to Center Road. All I want to do is lock my door and be alone, but the handle is broken.

My dad comes through the door.

"I'm sorry, Melissa," he says.

"I don't want to talk. I just want to be alone," I say.

Something is wrong between Eden and my dad. I pick up the paperweight with the golden lion I keep on my desk. A glass dome presses the gold lion safely against the black velvet background. I want to be like that lion, safe behind the thick glass.

"I'm sorry," my dad says again. "Your mother needs to have some goddamn involvement with you kids."

I've heard this from my dad before. But she's back living in Washington now. Things are out of control for my dad. I need to put the treasures in my room in order. I cup my hand over the dome of glass that protects the lion and say nothing to my dad.

"He tried to choke me. Jesus Christ, my own son tried to choke me. What the hell am I supposed to do?" he asks me.

I shrug my shoulders. I pull at the frayed threads along the bottom of my sweater pocket. I don't have the answers anymore. None of us do.

NOW

oh, bean

It was around this time that I began to spend more time away from the increasingly hostile environment of our big yellow house. The tension between my dad and Eden was explosive. Jamie discovered the outlet of hard drinking and vandalizing the town.

I suppose we were all destined to fall into drinking and experimenting with drugs. It was in our blood. Jamie was fearless. Eden was dangerous. I was silent. But we were losing our connection to one another. How I longed to be a tribe of three again. I wanted to sit with my brothers in the cool dirt underneath the house with boxes of cake mix—where we first tasted that sweet powder and were full of hope.

As I pull out more letters, I discover one my mom wrote but never sent to Eden around this time.

You really need to get out of your dad's house. I strongly believe any place is better for you than there—lotta heavy shit in that space. Oh my Bean, how hard it has been for you. How my heart has bled for you and continues to bleed. Maybe it's in my head as a penance for all my guilt about leaving you so long ago.

I have and will ever mourn the loss of my babies. Some say I "spared" myself the responsibilities of raising you—none will know the agonies of missing you. I still cry, but I know I did what I had to do, and the guilt must be continually held at bay, because it is worthless. How I wish my brother had lived— you are so like him, and he could have helped you be yourself. And of course, how I wish I could have been with you to encourage you and praise you. But my brother died and I was ill and I did suffer from it.

I feel such sadness for both my mom and brother in this letter. She is reaching out to him with such a rare kind of honesty. But she's wrong about my dad. When we were growing up, he never bad-mouthed her—and he protected us the best he could. We broke his heart over and over—and through it all, he was the one who stayed. From her letter, it seems her guilt was constantly lurking, causing her to hide her feelings from my brothers and me. I remember that feeling of hiding something—holding onto a secret—and hoping someone would rescue me.

THEN

lola asks

Here's how it starts.

I am turning the dial on my locker and there's Lola butting up to me. She's wearing her red velour V-neck and her tight Sticky Fingers jeans.

Her question catches me off guard. Way off guard. I keep turning the dial around and around because my fingers have suddenly forgotten the combination. I focus on the tiny black and white numbers ticking and spinning like a miniature raffle wheel in front of my face.

"Well?" she says.

"What? What'd you say?" I respond, even though I know exactly what she's asked me.

"I said do you want to get *wasted* tonight?"

Lola's lips are covered with thick, shiny lip gloss. She's so close I can smell it. It's roll-on Kissing Potion. Cola-flavored. Her large brown eyes dart back and forth with excitement behind her glasses.

My heart is kicking like a rabbit's foot. *Wasted.* Something Jamie says to his friends: "We're going out to get wasted Saturday night." Or maybe he says "shit-faced" or "hammered." I kind of get what it means. But not really.

"When? I mean how?" I ask.

Lola raises her voice as a group of ninth graders passes us. "With a couple six-packs of Schlitz." She smiles. "Suzee got her uncle to score for her. We're going to see this movie called *The Rocky Horror Picture Show* and we want to see it wasted."

Lola sounds as if she's won a sweepstakes. I look around to see who is overhearing this. Lola wants everyone to know that she is cool and in no way a "teamer." Teamers are cheerleaders and in sports and school clubs. Stoners hang out on the back field and get high.

So Lola isn't asking me to get stoned. She's asking me to get drunk. *Wasted.* She could have asked Amy Wright or Ellie Nichols but she's picking me. Probably because I'm not good at saying no.

"Yeah. Okay. Sure," I say. But my next thought is "Oh shit," and I'm wishing I had plans already or at least said I did.

"You can sleep over at my house too."

I push my locker closed and head across the quad to math class. *Wasted.* As I slip into my seat in Mr. Autry's algebra class, I keep repeating the word to myself just the way Lola said it with her eyes dancing back and forth. I know how other people act when they're that way, but I don't know what I will be like. Granted, it's not like I've never had alcohol before. I often have a sip of my dad's drinks—Myers's rum with Coke, Gallo red wine, and every kind of beer. I like the tastes. And I did drink a Coors tall when I was nine but it mostly made me tired. But I have never been *wasted*.

I don't want to be out of control like my dad's friends who come to our house and stay up all night. Or "mean Agnes," the person my dad told me that Mom turns into when she drinks too much. And I certainly don't want to be like any of my grandparents, who are all dead because they couldn't stop drinking.

But I kind of want to know what it feels like. Maybe I'm tired of being the goody-two-shoes all the time, holed up in my room to keep out the world. Maybe it would be good to lose control—just this once.

Mr. Autry, one of the teachers that I actually like in junior high, gives me a strange look—like he knows what I am going to do to tonight and he's worried about me. I can hear the chalk in his hand moving across the blackboard, but the only words I keep hearing are Lola's: "Melissa, do you want to get wasted tonight?" I imagine Mr. Autry pulling me aside after class and asking me if everything is all right. What would I say to him?

I rush out of class when the bell rings, holding on tight to the secret inside me.

My dad has the hose going in the garden. He holds his thumb halfway across the metal ring on the end, spraying it back and forth in an arc around him. He's quiet, thinking hard about something.

I lift a ripe lemon cucumber from the ground and pinch away its stem. It's one of the last left over from the summer.

"Dad? Lola wants to know if I can sleep over at her house tonight."

He keeps watering. "Tonight?"

"Yeah, 'cause it's Friday."

I want him to look at me. I want him to rescue me just this once. I want him to see a certain look in my gray eyes that tells him something is not right, that something inside me is wilting and I need his help. I want him to look at me and make a much better offer or just say, "No, not tonight," or "Let's go to Straw Hat and order a pineapple pizza."

But he doesn't.

He pulls the hose a little bit farther out. I focus on the garden. Those curly lettuces need an extra soak. And something is eating at the squash vines. I take a closer look. Small holes and Rorschach shapes pattern the wide green leaves. I watch the water from my dad's hose as it seeps into the dry ground and turns the soil dark and gritty, like coffee grounds. Here in our garden there are things that need tending to.

Maybe my dad is relieved that I have somewhere to go tonight. Maybe he's here because he needs some thinking time. But even in the calm of the garden, the skin is pulled tight across his jaw and there is a subtle but unmistakable tension in his posture as he moves the water back and forth. Things aren't easy these days. The yelling that goes on inside our house is constant. Jamie and Eden end up with Fs on every report card, suspensions from school, and restriction after restriction. And then there are the money problems that have been creeping under the floorboards like termites and words I overhear like "I'm going to lose this goddamn house if things don't change."

Finally he answers my question. "All right," he says. Just like that. No questions asked.

I look at him one more time in case he wants to change his mind. But all I hear is the sound of water hitting the earth. Tonight I can go out and get wasted with Lola. It's that easy. I wonder if it was this easy for Jamie and Eden too.

I walk back up to the house, pull a half carton of Neapolitan ice cream from the refrigerator, and head to my room. I lean up against my bed and shovel stripes of strawberry, vanilla, and chocolate into my mouth.

Our calico cat comes and sits at my feet as she always does when I have something to eat. She stares up at me with her big, gold-and-black eyes. I tell her what I'm about to do with Lola. I tell her that I'm scared but that it's too late and I'm going to do it anyway. Cats always listen. I let her lick the leftover vanilla off my spoon and fingers. Her small pink tongue is like a tab of fine sandpaper.

I stretch out across the floor in my room and stare up at the ceiling, feeling heavy and full, an overripe peach ready to fall from its branch.

———

We walk down the unlit alley behind the billiards hall to find the brown paper bag with the Schlitz beer. Lola, Suzee, and me. It's way cold out, and none of us are really dressed for this. We run our fingers along the chain-link fence, stepping on bits of broken glass.

"I really shouldn't be here," I say as we walk. "My dad has a workshop behind this alley."

"Melissa, your dad is not going to be working on a Friday

night," Lola says. I can tell she's getting irritated with me because I keep bringing up reasons why this might not be such a good idea.

"Don't be so straight," says Suzee.

"I'm not."

And so I don't bother mentioning that the Bit-a-Honey bar is across the street from the movie theater and my dad could easily show up there on a Friday night.

We find the brown grocery bag stashed behind the alley Dumpsters. Suzee leads us over to a small caged alcove with a No Trespassing sign and padlocks hooked onto heavy chains. It smells like urine.

"Just stay down on the ground when you see headlights come through the alley."

"But the sign says no…"

I stop myself from being called straight again. I don't particularly like Suzee. She's more Lola's friend than mine. She seems a lot older than us and wears way too much liquid eyeliner.

"This is so awesome," says Lola, grabbing a tall bottle of beer out of the bag.

She hands one to me. "Melissa, you get a better buzz if you drink it fast," says Lola.

"You're so skinny. You're probably like a complete lightweight," says Suzee.

I try throwing back a gulp like Suzee and Lola, but the cold bubbles make my throat burn.

"Truth or Dare, Suzee?" says Lola.

"Truth only," says Suzee.

"How far have you gone with a guy, Suzee?" asks Lola.

"Third."

"No way! I wouldn't even know how to do that," says Lola.

"It's not hard, Lola."

We sit chattering and swigging while Lola asks Suzee a million questions. I'm glad to just be quiet and listen. I feel the beer making my head a little dizzy.

Then Suzee turns to me. "Your brother Jamie is way cute."

Lola hands me another bottle.

"Truth, Melissa. How come you live with your dad and your brothers?"

"I don't know." I shrug. "My dad just decided to raise us, I guess."

"That's sort of fucked up, isn't it?" says Suzee.

Her words irritate me, and yet I can't seem to respond. I take another long drink of the beer and swirl it around in my mouth until it feels warm.

Lola jumps in. "Suzee, what gives? You're being kinda tight."

"No, it's just that I'd be pissed off if my mom wasn't around."

I want to say something, anything to try to explain, but my thoughts are running around too quickly for me to catch any particular one.

Lola and Suzee start talking about some of the girls that they can't stand at school, but I begin slipping into my own quiet, thinking world. The back of my throat feels numb. I've tried to do everything right, get good grades and be responsible. I promised myself that I would *never* do drugs, smoke, or drink—but here I am getting wasted.

And why shouldn't I be? Who really cares? Maybe I should be pissed off like Suzee says. Where is my mom these days anyway? Can she even imagine that I'm sitting here crouched in this alley drinking beer? Would it even bother her?

Maybe this is exactly where I should be—getting wasted in a dark alley. I look around, marveling at how all the bits of broken glass in the alley shimmer like tiny fish just beneath the surface of the water.

The beer warms me completely now. I can do whatever I want. I lift up my bottle and drink as fast and hard as I can.

"Right on, Melissa," says Suzee.

I look across the alley and think how easy it would be to throw my empty bottle against the concrete wall and listen as it smashes into a thousand pieces. I've carried this urge to break things for a long time but I've never had the guts do it. Now, finally, I raise my arm and hurl my beer bottle against the wall. The pitch is perfect. A sound that's beautiful and bad.

Lola looks at me wide-eyed, laughs out loud, and then throws her bottle.

I think I get it now why people break bottles in this dark alley. I know why Jamie has punched his fist through so much glass.

"You idiots," says Suzee. "You're so immature."

I don't care what Suzee says this time. We run down the alley, laughing, knowing we're already late for the movie because drinking the beer took longer than we thought. I am heavy and full of laughter, and it feels right.

The inside of the theater is dark and wobbles back and forth like we're on a boat. *The Rocky Horror Picture Show* is not a regular movie—people get out of their seats and dance and shout out loud. It's one of the weirdest things I've ever seen—and not because of the alcohol.

"Don't be surprised if you don't remember any of this tomorrow," says Suzee with her face pushed too close to mine. Someone next to me is shouting, "Dammit, Janet!"

I remember Janet. I don't remember how we got home.

If getting wasted means forgetting most of everything that happens in a night, then I did it right. And if Lola asks me again? I'll say yes.

THEN

hands

Aboyfriend appears suddenly, unexpectedly. He asks for my phone number at a party, and a week later, I've fallen into his world. His name is Hannon, and he attends the rival school across town. I was taken by his smile and his forwardness in asking for my phone number within minutes of meeting. I was also looking for some kind of change. Now, I'm not feeling so sure.

We're driving off county-maintained roads in Hannon's 442 Oldsmobile with white racing stripes on the hood. I ask him if he's ever been on these back roads.

"Yeah, once with my old girlfriend," he says.

He turns off the headlights, laughs, and says he can drive this road by Braille. I'm grateful for the full moon that's watching over us.

I'm not afraid of Hannon, but I'm uneasy that we're going to get stuck out here and I'll be home late again. He's brought me home late every time he's taken me out in his 442.

We park at the end of the dark road.

"Why are we stopping?" I ask.

"So we can be alone," he says, smiling.

"I can't be late again," I say. "My dad is going to kill me."

"Screw your dad. You're with me."

I can tell he's had too many beers by the edginess in his voice. He reaches under his seat, pulls out another can of Budweiser, and hands it to me.

"I'm okay."

"Are you kidding? Don't be a lightweight. Let's get wasted."

I don't want to get wasted. I want to talk about something other than getting drunk.

I flip on the interior light. I show him my hands. I make a fist to show him how the blue veins on the top of my left hand form a peace sign. I trace the outline of the symbol with my finger so he can follow.

"Cool," he says.

He starts kissing me in a way I don't want to be kissed. Sloppy and drunk. I pull away.

"You have to look at my hands."

"Why?"

"Please just look," I say.

I uncurl my fists as if I am revealing a secret. I lay my hands open for him to see—and for the first time he sees my flat palms covered with a map of intricate lines. Lifelines and heart lines going in every direction. Lines that normally don't appear on palms. More lines than on his mother's hands.

"Do you think there are too many lines?" I ask. I want him to look closely. I want him to admire them like rare etchings.

But he grabs my wrists. "I don't really care about your hands."

He pushes himself on top of me. Clumsy, with his pants on, he grinds against my hips. I lie still underneath him on the leather seat, closing my fists and wishing I hadn't made such a big deal about my hands. There is nothing special about them. I reach for the beer underneath the seat even though I don't want it. I'm out of things to offer. I'll get wasted and disappear into his world because I have nothing to lose anymore. I tilt my head back so I can see the sky above, the Little Dipper, and a million stars.

THEN

the good girl

The sharp gravel pushes into the arches of my bare feet. I hold my brown shoes and my purse against my chest to stop my heart from beating so hard. Getting safely across the gravel driveway that leads to our yellow house without being heard is close to torture at two o'clock in the morning. I've watched how our calico cat does it. Every step is low to the ground, measured and silent. Her eyes don't even blink as she threads her body through the grass. She's an expert but I have to stand for minutes at a time between each small movement here in the dark. Every step is a land mine of noisy, shifting gravel. It doesn't help that I'm drunk.

I am getting away with too much lately. I am as clever as my brothers now at creeping through the back windows late at night and telling lies, both the white kind and the black kind. I'm not one of the BPs (the beautiful people) at school because I don't hang out with those girls who have perfectly flipped hair and painted-on French jeans. And I don't hang around with the Ben Boys. They're so into their thin white T-shirts, steel-toed boots, and black Ben Davis pants. And I'm not a stoner like Jamie and his friends who practically own the back lot behind the gym, the creek, and the field at lunchtime. I may be uncategorized—a thin wisp of a girl looking for a role to play.

I take another step toward the yellow house and cross my fingers, hope to die that my dad is either not home or already asleep. I won't know until I get past the blackberry bushes, where I'll be able to see if his van is parked under the laurel tree. If it's not there, then it's a quick forty-second dash across the rest of the driveway, up the hillside, and in through the back door before he rolls in from the Bit-a-Honey downtown. If the van is parked under the laurel tree, then it's another twenty-minute cat creep across the gravel and in through the window.

I wait for a few minutes in the stretch of driveway between the overgrown blackberry thicket and the hedge of pink tea roses. This is where time always stops. Once I round this curve, everything changes and I am no longer protected by the branches of ripe fruit and the scent of a hundred flowers. Within this small stretch of space, between the blackberries and the tea roses, I wait as long as I can.

I'm supposed to be the good girl, the fair princess in the house of males. But I'm not. When I asked my dad what he would do if he found out that I started smoking cigarettes (which I don't), he didn't pause. He didn't hesitate. "I'd disown you," he said.

I asked him why it was okay for everyone else, including Jamie and Eden, to smoke but not me.

"Because you're different. You're smarter than that," he said.

That's what pisses me off the most. What makes him think I'm so different? Why shouldn't I be as messed up as the rest of us? I'm jumping off the pier with my brothers. We're holding hands, sinking down into the soft sand underwater. Lola asks, *Melissa, you want to get high after school? Okay, sure.* My boyfriend asks, *Melissa, you want do some lines of cocaine at the drive-in? All right.* I keep my thoughts and answers simple because I don't want to think or feel too much.

There is something good about being numb. The dentist slowly pushes in that long needle of Novocain for a reason. My boyfriend hands me a small mirror lined with clean, white lines of powder for that same reason. He also tells me I'm a lightweight and a cheap date because I don't require much. My skinny frame has its limit. I cheat on a test if I need to because I'm not naturally smart like Lola. I've learned how to slip almost microscopic cheat sheets into the taped cuffs of my jeans.

I say yes to every party and make sure I slam a beer quickly so that I can feel the buzz as soon as possible. At first I just drank keg beer, but now Jell-O shots and cocaine are lined up in the back rooms of these parties and I get invited in. I'm not the one who rolls up the dollar bill; I'm just the one who uses it. It's always free. I rub the leftover flakes into my gums. Numbness feels great.

I try not to think about my actions and take an uneven step around the corner. Fully lit, our big yellow farmhouse stares down at me in disapproval. The van is not under the laurel tree, but someone's car is here. A green Chevy Nova parked sideways beneath the oak tree that belongs to one of Jamie's Ben Boy friends. They usually hang out downstairs drinking and smoking pot if my dad isn't home.

I quicken my pace toward the window to my bedroom, now knowing that the headlights from my dad's van could come around the corner any second, knowing that whoever is here could suddenly walk out the front door. I need to slip into my room without being detected. These days, more than ever, I need the shelter of my room, where the world feels contained and in order.

I can still be the good girl, I think. If only everything outside of the yellow house wasn't moving so fast.

I lift up the window to my room. The old panes hesitate from too many layers of paint. The window halfway open, I slide my stomach over the sill and land with a quiet thump inside my room with a sigh of relief. I feel like Alice in Wonderland. I'm looking for the label that says "Drink Me." I'm looking for the key to that tiny door. I want to be small again.

NOW

solitude

It's past midnight. I check in with Kim, who is still awake, to see if he needs help with anything. A pair of wire-rimmed glasses rests on the bridge of his nose, and a second pair is perched on top of his head. He lifts his eyes from the pages of his paperback and shakes his head, the picture of strength. "No, everything is okay for now."

I'm glad my mom has this stoic man by her side.

"Good night, Mom," I say from the doorway.

I walk upstairs and call my husband and explain that she's still hanging in there.

"You can stay longer if you need to," he says to me.

"I can't. I don't know what the right thing to do is anymore."

"What's going on?"

"I miss you guys."

"We miss you too."

When I hang up, I feel irritable. As tough as these last days with my mom are, I know that I have to switch roles as soon as I return home. I will lose the solitude I have had here. Instead, I will be consumed by housework and tending to what the kids need—the cleaning, scheduling, getting them to and from school, buying their school supplies, making their meals, organizing their visits with friends, paying the bills, and playing the part of the tooth fairy, the Easter bunny, the toilet cleaner, the laundry maker.

The house is sure to be a complete mess when I return. It's a domestic battle that I lose every day. As much as I want to tell the kids and Anthony to clean up their crap, it's easier for me just to do it myself. The filthy kitchen counters and the whole goddamn kitchen itself are enough to drive a parent mad.

I imagine that most mothers—even if just for a fleeting moment when the kids are screaming and your spouse is being a jerk and the bills are late again and you're just desperate for a moment of peace—at some point long to just drop everything and pick up a new life, a calm life, a free life to pursue their passions and ideas without any responsibilities to tie them down.

Right now though, it's late, and I need to decide whether to stay or leave Olympia. I don't want to be angry with my mom but I am. I resent that she has pulled me away from my family during Christmas. I've been completely detached from my kids since I've arrived. And I know it's not her fault or intention, but the anger in me is rising.

I should be screaming at myself for being a coward. I selfishly wanted to be next to her when she closed her eyes and stopped breathing. I childishly wanted to hold her hand, thinking it would make up for all the years she wasn't there to hold mine. But I know now that I'm not going to be here for that moment. Even so, I want nothing more now than for her to die while I'm still here. Not in two days, not in twelve. Here and now.

THEN

clear lake

I'm seventeen, sitting in the slippery backseat of a beat-up orange Camaro with my boyfriend and a couple guys I hardly know. Hannon is trying to impress them with his altered California ID. I can't tell if I'm feeling carsick or just tired of this endless game of getting high. When I was nine, I'd sometimes watch the pink-eyed mice in the window at Scooter's Pet Shop frantically spinning on their wheels and wonder if they understood they weren't going anywhere at all. That's how I'm feeling now.

I didn't particularly want to go on this overnight trip, but Hannon said that we might have a chance to water-ski on the lake and that's something I'd love to do. From the minute we left Novato, the driving has been nothing less than reckless. We're speeding close to sixty around tight one-lane roads, the guys cheering when the tires screech. I anchor my elbow into the armrest and close my eyes each time the car flies around the sharp turns.

"Don't worry. I know where the cops stake out this road," says the guy behind the wheel.

He pumps the brakes, rocking us back and forth as we pull into a gas station halfway up the mountain. One more stop to score another twelve-pack and stock up on Red Vines candy.

Hannon shoves his fake ID into his wallet and jumps out of the car with giddiness in his step. His friend Marty follows, with a baseball cap pulled down to his eyebrows.

"I'm going to head across the street," I say. But they don't hear me.

A sign that says "Antiques" in hand-painted gold letters is calling my name.

"What are you doing?" Hannon yells to me.

"I just want to take a look. Real quick. I promise." The wind pushes my gauze skirt up as I cross the road.

When I open the door to the shop, the scent of furniture polish and musty paper invites me in. French wax, lemon oil, and Wright's Silver Cream—the familiar smells from my father's first antique store in Santa Rosa. The woman behind the counter nods at me and smiles politely.

There are oak tables with feet carved like lion's paws, brass lamps, stacks of leather-bound books, and colorful glassware lighting up the windowsill and throwing prisms of color across the floor. I suddenly want to be lost here in the quiet space. Pink and yellow Depression glass, cranberry and cobalt vases. I miss the days when I would spend hours exploring my dad's shop, discovering the hidden drawers inside of antique desks and imagining the things I could stow away in them.

I set my hand against the glass of a lighted showcase filled with a collection of paperweights. The colorful millefiori catches my attention—a compact arrangement of delicate pink and sapphire-blue flowers surrounded by vibrant green stalks and leaves.

"Millefiori. Italian for a million flowers," my dad taught me a long time ago. I love the idea of a million flowers all contained inside the glass.

Hannon raps his fist against the outside of the shop window. I don't want to get back in the car and drive to Clear Lake.

"We're going. Come on!" he yells.

Goddamn it. I wish we weren't so far from home.

I wedge myself into the backseat. Before I can even buckle my seat belt, the orange Camaro squeals out of the gas station. The driver, Jay, looks back at me from his rearview mirror. His eyes are deep green and sandy, like the kelp that my brothers and I used to pull from the water at Agate Beach. He asks me if I like antiques.

"I do," I say.

"Yeah, me too," he says. "I love that old stuff with a history."

Wow, this guy might be more interesting than I imagined. Before our conversation even starts, Hannon, hardly discreet, reaches behind me and snaps open my bra.

"You don't need that thing on," he says. "Marty, here, will agree."

I cast him an angry look and he laughs at me. His laughter pulls at the back of my neck with the tension of a taut slingshot. I fall silent again and turn my attention to everything outside the car—the blur of redwoods and pines, the late-afternoon sun blinking and finally setting behind us.

It's dark by the time we pull into a narrow dirt driveway. The cabin in Clear Lake is not what I expected. There are bare bulbs hanging from yellow electrical cords, a few pieces of furniture, and several thin mattresses tossed on the floor. Jay explains that it's kind of a party pad until his parents get the flooring and plasterboard in.

"This is fucking awesome!" Hannon calls out. His voice echoes through the empty rooms of the house. "This is like the ultimate place to get hammered, dude."

Hannon and Marty are slaphappy, checking out the place.

"We've even got a brew freezer," says Hannon, high-fiving Marty and Jay. He's an idiot when it comes to drinking.

Hannon tosses a can of beer at me from across the room. I let it fall on the flimsy mattress at my feet. I want to be a thousand miles from here, and I don't know how to say it.

In the bathroom, I apply a line of black eyeliner and paint my lips with tinted lip gloss. I catch my distorted reflection in the cabinet mirror propped up against the shower stall. My mom told me that it's "unfortunate" I inherited my father's nose, but that I could always get it "bobbed" when I turn eighteen. If she hadn't said that, I might feel okay about my nose. It's my entire body that I hate lately.

I want to change. I want something to wake me up. I don't want to be with this guy. But I am the one who packed a toothbrush, a change of clothes, and a new stick of black eyeliner, and then stepped into the orange Camaro. I am the one who lied to my dad and told him I was spending the night at a girlfriend's house.

Hannon bangs on the door. "I need to take a piss," he says.

I'm not friendly to him. It's freezing in this shitty cabin.

"Why aren't you out here getting hammered?" he says. "Come on, drink up."

"I don't really feel like it."

"Whoa, what's up with you?"

I walk past him outside to the porch and he follows. A layer of thick fog has surrounded the cabin since we arrived. The tall pines overhead rustle in the dark like the spirits of old men.

I am precise with my words. "I'm getting tired of this whole getting-wasted thing. Is that what you really like? Is that all you want to do?"

"Fuck yeah. That's what we came here for."

"Well, I'm not sure that's what I want anymore."

"Well, what do you want then?"

This is always where I chicken out. The question that silences me.

"I don't know. Maybe I just want to go home."

He laughs. "Well you're shit out of luck on that." His cockiness warns me that the alcohol has already settled in.

"Home?" he says. "I mean *what the fuck* is at home for you? Your dad is most likely out drinking at the bars. Hammered. Your mom doesn't even live in the same state. She's so smart that she knows every word in the dictionary. But remind me again, what is she doing now? Is she still sticking labels on tuna cans? And your brothers? They're going off the fuckin' deep end."

"It wasn't tuna, Hannon. She's a cocktail waitress now."

"Damn," he continues. "You ever heard that saying that the apple never falls far from the tree? You think you're something special?"

He knows how to snap my ribs without even hitting them. I look up at the sky for visible stars that might save me from believing his words. I can smell his breath, predict what's coming next. He moves in close to me. "I've got to train you better."

I've heard this speech so many times. How he "trained" his parents to respect him and now he's got to train me. I hate that I don't fight back. But I am the peacekeeper, the nice girl, the skinny toothpick holding up the whole house where my dad and brothers and I live.

Jay swings the door open. "You guys coming in or what?"

Hannon looks at me. "Suit yourself, but I'm going to get drunk and have fun—fun with a capital F."

I sit down on the makeshift mattress-couch and watch the three of them laughing, drinking, and passing a joint back and forth. The dinner is cheese puffs, Red Vines, and a tub of pepperoni sticks. I tell Hannon that I will have a beer after all, and he brings me an open can from the freezer. I sip on it just to keep the peace while the guys launch into a rowdy game of quarters. Maybe if there were another girl here, things wouldn't be as bad. Jay says his girlfriend ditched out at the last minute. Then again, I'm used to being the only girl. I live in a house of boys.

Hannon gets up, plants a sloppy kiss on my mouth, and runs his hand along my waist.

"How are you feeling? Did you like that beer?" he asks. He takes the can out of my hand and tilts it back and forth.

"There are still a couple more sips in here." He's smirking. "I put something special in it for you—a little upper to keep you happy." He squeezes my thigh tightly.

I want to jump up and hit him. But then I think he must be lying.

"Please tell me you wouldn't do that."

"Just a little something." He winks. "It won't hurt you."

My body starts shaking. And then my stomach curls into a knot. I want to vomit. I should punch him in the mouth.

"You fucking bastard!"

The room is silent. All three of them stare at me. I stand up and walk toward the door, trying to contain myself. When I reach for the doorknob, I can see myself in two places at once. I'm sitting with the guys back on the striped mattress. But I'm also standing in front of the door. It's like I got up too quickly and walked out of my body. I stand still for a second or two, wondering how to reconnect myself, how to snap my parts back together. And then I walk out of the cabin with no idea where I'm going. I don't care if I get lost this time.

I hear Hannon's voice trailing, "Don't worry. She's fine. She just needs to mellow out."

My high heels clack against the pavement on the main road. Who the fuck does he think he is, tricking me, putting something into my drink to alter my state? He's held onto me by belittling me constantly—threatening that if I ever tried to break up with him, he would simply "erase me" from his mind. He said it would take him exactly two weeks, and then it would be as if I never existed.

The problem is, I'm weak. I'm desperate for someone to like me, approve of me, stay with me. I wanted a boyfriend so badly that I took the first offer that came along. Doesn't matter that it also happened to be the crappiest offer. He likes to remind me that I could never do any better than him.

The sound of my heels clicking in the stillness of the night starts to unnerve me. I pick up my shoe and rub my finger along the bottom where the metal point has pushed through the white leather. I put the shoe back on and move toward the dirt path alongside the road. Headlights creep up from behind me like a stage spotlight. I won't turn around because I'm not going to talk to him or his fucked-up friends. The headlights grow wider and fill the landscape with light. I refuse to turn my head, refuse to be mocked. The noisy engine edges up almost parallel to me.

"You lost, sweetheart?"

It's a man's voice. A voice I have never heard.

I turn my head and am startled by the paleness of the man's face staring at me. A man with thick lips and a deep, receding hairline—skin that looks as though it has never seen sunlight. He looks almost familiar.

"Can I offer you a ride?"

I don't stop walking or change my pace.

His car is a long, maroon sedan of some sort. A Buick or a Plymouth. What does it matter really? I smell the gasoline fumes as he idles alongside me. A Pontiac, maybe? I am acutely aware of how I must appear, walking alone down the road on a chilly night. I've got on a pair of scuffed-up white pumps, a thin gauze skirt, and a tiny sweater with no bra.

"No, that's all right," I say.

"You look like you're lost, Little Sheba," he says.

Did he *really* just call me that? So maybe he's a creep, but what if this is a chance to actually catch a ride out of here? When my mom used to pick up hitchhikers, it would scare the hell out of me. She said she'd look carefully at their eyes and use her best judgment before letting them in the car. I don't recall her ever turning someone down. What else did she consider in those moments before making her decision?

I take another glance. And then I realize what's familiar about him. He looks like the Joker from the *Batman* episodes my brothers used to watch after school. A chill runs up my spine. I'm not getting in the car with the Joker.

"I'm just walking home," I say.

If I keep my feet moving and keep talking to him, I can to get to the next lot where there's a cabin.

"Do you live around here?" I ask.

"Sort of," he says.

My breath is erratic and visible. I'm wondering what exactly was in that pill anyway. Is it just the mystery pill that's got my heart pounding?

Keep walking. Keep talking to the Joker.

A yellow light ahead, a single halo on a wrap-around porch.

"Get in," he says.

"I live right here. I'll see you. Later."

And I'm sprinting like a deer across the grass and toward the light. His car stays idling on the side of road. I can feel him watching my back, waiting to see if I walk in that front door. I can't knock and have nobody answer, so I step onto the porch and then run toward the back of the cabin. Crouched beneath a darkened window, I grab onto my arms to stop them from shaking.

Half a minute and I creep off the porch to the woods behind the house. I keep moving, my heels pushing into the soft dirt, my hand touching the branches of trees as I walk. I travel backward in the direction that I came from, staying away from the main road because I never want to see that creep again. I imagine him tricking me just like Hannon tricked me, this Joker showing up on the trail in front of me, grabbing me, pushing me down into the earth, my hand grabbing at the dark soil, my scream silenced by the stars.

I still my thoughts and quicken my pace.

It is the orange Camaro sitting like a tiger in the overgrown grass that tells me I have found my way back to the cabin.

I sit outside on the steps of the deck, shaking and cold, but afraid to go in. This night has been all about being in the wrong places. I know this. There are lyrics from The Beatles playing in my head—"Nothing's gonna change my world." All my spinning thoughts come down to a single sentence. I repeat it to myself so that I will never forget it. *This is not what I want. This is not what I want.*

The back door opens. It's Jay.

"Hey, you're back."

I stay glued to the porch steps.

"You ought to come in. Hannon is totally passed out."

Thank God, I think to myself and stand up. Jay stands in the doorway, his shadow filling the frame. He must be pretty drunk.

"You are beautiful. You know that?" he says, moving closer to me. I look up at him. His green eyes, kind and surprisingly focused, rearrange my thoughts. Nobody has ever called me beautiful.

Beautiful is *not* a person. It's an object in an antique store, a pink tea rose, a hillside covered with buttercups. All at once, I am a thousand flowers beneath the glass. A millefiori.

"Beautiful," he repeats. There is heat coming off his body and I want nothing more than to be warm. I let him kiss me with his drunk, sweet lips. I'm kissing the wrong guy. He has a girlfriend. He moves his hands across the skin of my back like he's putting the final polish on his fender. *Nice*, I think. I let him kiss me some more.

He lifts my chin and says, "Man, you deserve better than that jerk."

"Thanks," I say.

"I can't stand up anymore. You want to lie down with me?" he asks.

I kiss him again. "No, I can't. Maybe someday though."

He staggers into the cabin and falls onto an empty mattress.

I crawl to the space opposite Hannon and lie down on my back. His mouth hangs open like a Venus flytrap waiting to snatch its prey. But he also looks harmless, the way he sleeps with his hands quiet and curled near his chin. No, he's still a jerk.

Wide awake, I stare at the dark wooden beams above me. I stretch my arms out across the mattress as if they are wings that could carry me to another place. Something inside me is creaking open like an old iron gate that has been wrought with vines and rust for a long time. Nothing touches me as I close my eyes—not my clothes, not the cold air, not the mattress beneath me. I am floating out of this place and into another place, a better place. Because an apple *can* fall far from the tree. *Because this is not what I want.*

NOW

darkness

Instead of going back upstairs, I push open the screen door and exit my mom's blue house. I need to walk, to feel my feet against the hard winter ground, and shake the numbness from my body. The field where the ponies roam is three hundred yards away. I venture into the darkness with only the moon as my light. For all I know, I could be standing outside the cabin in Clear Lake twenty-five years ago. But I am here outside my mom's house where the cold air blankets my body and reminds me how alive I am in this moment. My mom won't ever experience this sensation again. Is this what it feels like right now for her? Is she stepping out into the dark or the light?

I feel my mom here with me under the stars. I lie down on my back and stare up at the sky. I am not afraid. This ground will hold me up. This same ground will swallow my mother's body. I suppose I will always be the girl looking for answers in the stars and the bent trees overhead. If I had the fortitude, I'd pull myself off the ground and go shake my mom awake and tell her how much I love her. But I can't yet.

I lie still in the pasture, listening to the sound of the ponies breathing and the leaves rustling. I remember the feeling of being eight months pregnant with my first baby—my belly full and taut, my insides being kicked and pulled and stretched. The sensation was both magical and frightening. I imagine my mom lying down in an open field like this with me kicking around in her belly. What did she hope for? Was it too frightening for her? How strange it is to imagine that I once swam in the warm darkness of her belly. Her eyes were the first I knew and trusted. Here in the night field, grass and earth beneath my body, I listen for my mother's heartbeat. Her breath and mine, connected. What else is there left to do except open myself to every possibility?

By the time I pull myself from the ground, my whole body is cold and I hurry back inside the blue house. Upstairs, with my mom's letters in hand, I find myself wondering what kind of mother I will be when my children hit adolescence. What will my children say about me? That I held them too tightly? Or that I let them fly from the nest on crooked wings?

For several years during my adolescence, my mom became even more distant. Maybe it was difficult for her to suddenly see her little girl growing into a young woman. Maybe I was pushing her away.

A letter titled "Dear Mommy" sits in the file of letters never sent. Maybe one of the letters my mom wrote while she was in rehab—since it's a letter written many years after her mother died.

Dear Mommy,

I try to remember you ever holding me, and I can't. Who'd want to hold a brat? I remember spitting at you after you spanked me. I also remember thinking how beautiful and perfect you were—until I was ten or so and I saw your lipstick was on crookedly one Christmas in Florida. And I hated you and felt pity for you after David was killed.

Have I always missed having a mother? How many horse shows did you come to, Mommy? [None.] How many riding lessons was I late for because you were not into taking me— or not into me, period? You were always sleeping through my nightmares unless Jo woke you up.

We won't even mention the years of your drunkenness. You were gone then—really gone. Get your spirit together and help me for once in this life. Release me. Please, please, please. I know you weren't a very happy person—you had so many demons. I am sorry—really I am. But I have suffered your demons, and I am tired, tired, tired. Please help.

Your daughter,
Mikel

History repeats itself again and again. The past and present collide in my mother's words. Daughters never stop longing for their mothers. So where does this thread of broken mothers begin and end? And if it's true that things are fated to repeat themselves, what did I think I would find different here in Olympia?

I think about my brothers and wish they could be here to say good-bye with me. We share this history of longing for our dazzling mother.

Around the time Jamie, Eden, and I were old enough to leave the nest of our big yellow house, our dad's financial situation had spun out of control. He was heavily in debt and in danger of losing the house and everything else he owned. None of us were ready to say good-bye to the house that had held us for so many years.

The day of the auction, I learned that the things that matter to people can so easily end up in the wrong hands. In our yellow house, the things all disappeared in a single day.

THEN

the cost of a blue chair

Downstairs, everything from our yellow house is neatly laid out in categories. Bidding numbers are attached like toe tags to each item. Grandma Rita's china and silver have been moved out of the dark oak cabinet and stacked onto sale tables in Jamie's room. Pictures and paintings have been taken off the walls and placed on upright easels. Smaller items have been organized into group lots. The powder-blue fish plates in Lot 49 are stacked high with their tails and fins going in mismatched directions.

"Those are Limoges," I hear someone say behind me.

Pretending to be a shopper, I slide my fingers across each item and note its lot number. I stop in front of my grandmother's dessert plates, each one hand-painted with a different kind of flower—red poppies, yellow roses, pink cherry blossoms, black-eyed Susans, white lilies, and blue forget-me-nots. A set of six. My dad told me once that those were his mother's favorite plates. They were mine too. I thought that they would always be stacked there in the dark wood cabinet, waiting for me to use if I ever had a family of my own.

A trifold flyer for the day's event has fallen to the floor, and I stare at it in disbelief. The auctioneer helped my dad design it. The bold, black print reads:

PUBLIC AUCTION. COMPLETE ESTATE OF
1735 CENTER ROAD. RAIN OR SHINE.

EVERYTHING GOES…TO THE BARE WALLS!

On the flyer are black-and-white photos of our furnishings— paintings, carpets, Victorian lamps, dressers, desks, the stained-glass windows, and the ice-cream-parlor table and chairs. Certain items for sale on the flyer have stars and exclamation points as if they are more important.

I should have been paying more attention. I should have taken my dad's word when he told me that all he had left were the coins on the dashboard of his van. He said not to worry because he was going to work things out "no matter what," and I trusted him. After all, he was my dad, and he had always stuck by us, always worked things out for us one way or the other.

I knew things were getting worse when the power and water kept getting shut off month after month. Whenever PG&E called to say our electricity was going to be turned off by 5 p.m. if the bill wasn't paid, my dad would tell me to say the same thing: "Tell them to just put the check back through."

I didn't understand what that meant, but I knew it rarely worked. Sometimes eating dinner by candlelight with candles flickering all around us was magical. We argued less and talked more softly. When the power was restored, the spell was broken.

On the long table in Jamie's room I notice Grandma's set

of fancy cordial glasses with the twisted stems. Each one is a different color—rose, lavender, and icy blue—the colored glass as thin as puddle ice in spring. Even Boris, the stuffed wild-pig head, is to be sold. Almost every friend of mine has touched his pink shellacked tongue on a dare.

Our 1965 *Collier's Encyclopedia* set and the *Great Books* are stacked in two tall towers and numbered. I open one of the encyclopedias and flip to the color plates in the center. I look at "Birds of the World" and "Mammals of the Americas" one last time.

Then, from across the room, I spot her slender arms reaching toward the sky, her face still smiling. A number in bold, black ink dangles from her wrist. Item 152, the Good Fairy, the small metal statue my dad brought home from the antique fair so many years ago. The floor beneath my feet seems to shift as if I have missed a step. She is my favorite thing in our yellow house. Like me, she is a young girl cast in a single moment with her arms outstretched wide and standing on her tiptoes.

It's not right to sell the Good Fairy. The first time I noticed her in the windowsill in my father's room, I felt such hope—like I too could reach out beyond the borders of our yellow house. I wonder if anyone would notice if she went missing from the auction, if I shoved her under my coat and walked away with her. But that would be a stupid thing to do when my dad is trying so hard to get enough money to save our house.

My dad told each of us to set aside our "necessary" things from our bedrooms so they wouldn't end up in the auction.

"Antiques can be bought and sold and replaced. It's that simple," he says.

My friend Rhonda, whose mother makes her bed every morning after she leaves for school, asked me if I was mad about my dad putting on an auction to sell all the stuff in our house. "What would you rather have? Your house or all the things in it?" I asked her.

"Both," she said.

She just doesn't get it. And why would she? It's not a choice she has to make. *I* get it because I know I can't change things. I feel bad for my dad. This is not what he wants; it is what he has to do to save our house.

Quickly, I turn away from the Good Fairy, bumping my hip against the corner of a table. Nothing is where it usually is. Overnight our house has been transformed into a crowded shop—not unlike my dad's antique shop. In the living room, I sit in my grandmother's blue chair—the big easy chair with its down cushions and deep, low seat that came to us the summer after she died. My brothers and I still fight over who gets to sit in the blue chair because it is, we have all decided, the most comfortable chair in the whole world.

I sink down into its soft cushions and set my elbow against one of its big arms as I study the faces of people milling about. They look greedy, every one of them, a flock of magpies flapping from room to room, circling over our stuff. What do they really want with our things anyway? Do they understand that no one has died here but that they're taking from us as we watch them scavenge?

A man in a corduroy sports coat looks down at me and smiles broadly. "How's that chair? It sure looks comfortable," he says.

"No, not really," I reply.

I stand up and walk out on the upstairs balcony. Down below, beneath the big oak tree in the yard, are rows of folding chairs, red and white balloons, free beer, and strangers clutching lists of the items they will bid on. I feel transparent—a ghost girl, wandering from room to room in a house I once skipped through.

The auctioneer who my dad hired wears a constant smile as he watches the steady stream of people arriving. More people, the "right" kind of people, mean a bigger commission in his pocket. My dad must be relieved about the turnout as well. The auction is his last card. He recently had to rescue our yellow house from being auctioned off on the front steps of City Hall.

He's explained that he has a debt to pay, and if he sells everything on the inside of the house, he might have enough to pay the bank off before they try to take the house from us again. I don't completely understand the details, but I know that my dad has been borrowing money from a lot of people to get himself out of this mess.

"Don't worry, Melissa. I'm not going to let you down," he tells me this time.

I don't know what's going to happen if we lose our yellow house. Jamie dropped out of high school to join the marines, so I don't see him much these days because he's in training camp. Eden comes and goes between our house and different friends' homes. My mom is back living in Washington with a new boyfriend. Last I talked to her, she said that my dad ought to set the house on fire and collect the insurance money if he truly wants to get out of the situation.

When all the folding chairs are filled, the auctioneer takes center stage on our front porch. He's a slick cowboy with snake-skin boots and a black-and-brown-plaid shirt. His stomach bulges over the ledge of his silver belt buckle. As he takes command of the crowd, his voice booms into the microphone. His way of speaking is slippery and fast. I spy Eden standing in the back row with his arms crossed. The bidding begins in a frenzy, cardboard numbers jumping high over heads of buyers like determined salmon spawning upstream.

I don't expect Eden to be upset once the bidding begins because he is the one who has always complained about the "stupid and useless antiques" in our house. "What good are things you have to be so damn careful with?" he always says. He hates the fact that our dad sells antiques to make a living. He likes things new and modern—and he reminds us of this all the time. Yet, when the bidding begins, Eden is the one who is desperate. He runs between the rows of folding chairs.

"Dad, what are you doing? You can't sell all this…It's going too cheap!"

I can see it in his face. He wants to save everything, but it is all happening too fast.

Eden marches to the back row of chairs and holds a bidding number high in the air for the small Maxfield Parrish painting of the lady standing in the bright, blue water. The auctioneer ignores his number and gives the Parrish to the high bidder in the first row. Standing behind the people, Eden begins a rant.

"Can you believe this shit? This is my grandma's! And that is my dresser and my desk. And those are our family heirlooms. Jeez, how can you even watch this? This is not right."

There are times when I wish I had the guts to be bold like

Eden—to rant, to yell, to call it like it is. But I turn inward and go silent. I am the watcher, the one whose voice is still tangled in her throat.

My dad marches across our gravel driveway and pulls Eden out of the crowd. "What are you doing, being a smart-ass out there? Since when are you interested in antiques?"

Eden yanks his arm away. "This is a circus, Dad! And you're the clown here, man."

My dad doesn't yell. Instead, he calmly looks at Eden while his hands twitch close to his sides as if to say, *What can I do?* He sighs. "You can't bid on anything unless you have the money to pay for it, Eden. People here are going to get angry, and you need to start saving money to live on your own."

Eden stares straight ahead at the stage as if he's going to charge the front porch. "I got some money to get a few things."

"Please, sit down or else you need to leave."

At that moment, I look away from Eden's face, so I don't know why he suddenly chooses to stop fighting. I want to focus on what's coming and going on the front porch. I need to watch the things go so that I can remember them. A familiar sadness creeps inside me. How do you say good-bye to things you love? You don't really. You just watch and hope they will come back someday.

Eden and I sit in fold-up chairs and watch everything disappear, lot by lot. Two smartly dressed men sitting a few rows from us bid on almost every item and pay top dollar, which makes me feel oddly grateful but also hate them. It's like they are going to furnish a whole house to look just like ours.

An antique dealer hurries away down our gravel driveway

with a tea set and a box of our grandmother's silver. My favorite painting of the cowboy in his yellow hat is gone in less than sixty seconds. The 1940s calendar print of the starlet with bare shoulders and candy-apple red lips brings more than a hundred dollars.

When the Good Fairy comes onto the porch, I turn away from the house. I don't want to know what price she brings. I tell myself that I don't care—that I'm being too girlish in wanting to keep a fairy. When I look back toward the porch, I only see her outstretched arms as she is carted off in a flimsy cardboard box.

By late afternoon many of the bidders are gone. With the less valuable pieces remaining, the prices begin to drop. Despite my dad's wishes, Eden starts bidding again, but he mainly throws up a number to "up" the prices so things don't go so cheaply. It's not legal to do this. He claims he's got a stash of money from selling pot at school.

Then the blue chair is carried onto the porch, the blue chair that came to us after Grandma Rita died. The blue chair that we all agree is the most comfortable chair in the world.

The bid opens at eight dollars.

"Eight dollars!" says Eden. "Shit, that's nothin'."

My dad is nowhere in sight.

I don't really think it through. I raise my hand, even though I don't have a number.

Then Eden's hand shoots up. And then the man's hand in front of us goes up. We are all bidding on the blue chair.

"You don't even have a number," says Eden.

"Eden, please let me use your number just this once. I'll get the money and pay you back," I say.

"But I want that chair," he says.

"Do I hear twelve dollars?"

"Who will give me fourteen dollars for this cozy old chair?"

I grab Eden's number and keep my hand raised high.

The price keeps going up.

"Twenty-two? Can I get twenty-two?"

The man in front of me turns to his friend and says, "Just let the girl have the chair."

When the auctioneer says, "Sold to the young lady," I think he's joking.

For a second, Eden gets mad at me, but then I catch the corners of his mouth turning slightly like he is glad.

"That's alright," he says. "I got the painting of the swans when Dad wasn't paying attention."

Was it really this easy? Why hadn't I bid on other things— like the Good Fairy?

I paid twenty-two dollars for our grandmother's blue chair.

My dad doesn't mention anything about my purchase but I know he knows about it. He and the auctioneer celebrate the success of the auction over a lot of rum and red wine. They have good reason to celebrate. The auction was a success, which means my dad can probably pay whoever he needs to pay.

I wake up later in the night and find my way to the blue chair, which has been pushed to the far end of the porch. I drop myself down into it and pull my legs up close to my chest. Everything is quiet except for the wind that rustles through the leaves of our giant, old oak tree. The first time I skipped across the porch of this yellow house, I knew it was a good house. It was the one solid thing beneath my feet. A nest, a mother, a yellow house. I remember what I said to Jamie the first day we were here.

"Isn't this the greatest place we ever lived, Jamie?"

"I think it is. I think it is," he said back.

He was right. Even with almost nothing in it, the house still feels like our castle.

There are some things I instinctively know. I can't always explain, but it's as clear as can be: we will lose the yellow house after all.

It is only a matter of time before we will say good-bye. We will lose the barn, the blackberries, the pink tea roses, the garden, the lilacs, and the very earth that we have traveled across every day.

What would you rather lose? Your house or everything in it?
Neither.

Someday I'm going to find the Good Fairy in the back of an antique shop, and I'll buy her no matter what she costs. I will seek out all the treasures that left our yellow house. I will frequent antique stores, curiosity shops, and flea markets where I will look into silver teapots in hopes of seeing my grandmother's reflection. I will rummage through boxes of sterling in hopes of finding a copy of her Victorian cranberry spoon. I will line a cupboard with hand-painted flower plates. I will not forget the way my favorite painting of the cowboy always hung slightly crooked in our hallway.

I sit in the blue chair and tell myself one more time that things aren't supposed to matter. People can be unreliable. People leave. But the things were supposed to stay.

NOW

a thousand places at once

I keep rereading her letters. I am the fool still searching for something that will give me some fragment of closure—that one sentence that tells me why she left. I come across a letter she never sent to Bill, the horse trainer from Texas. Her love affair with him almost broke my parents apart the first time. And there were many others along the way too. Perhaps she left because she loved another man.

Dear Bill,

Whatever prompted me to call? Perhaps it is because the day I spent with you made me realize exactly what it is like to be free and single and twenty-one. And how I long to be free! Maybe I just want to avoid all responsibility. I don't know. But I am so full of desire to be a thousand places at once, to do exactly as I feel—to be exhilarated by my life instead of bearing with it. As to what I'm going to do now? First of all, get away from the complete chaos around me.

By hook or by crook, I'm going off by myself for at least two weeks of thought and rest. Something has always come up to show me what a compensation I am living. Except always in the past I've turned up pregnant and have had to stay— and pregnancy is a panacea for all ills. No babies going now though—I should add "unless it's yours" and scare you half to death, but jacks are jacks and I'm as good as sterile.

In actuality you are the very nemesis of my soul—whatever nebulous thing that may be—saturated and suffocated by a love that really has no right to be. So what to do? Somewhere there is a place for me, a time when I can be happy with myself.

Later—So running off to Texas with you would be the most God-awful step I could take—though it certainly wasn't very nice of you to tell me so.

Oh Mom, I think your heart never knew which way to go. Why was it so hard to stay in one place, or even if that was too much, to be a reliable presence in your children's lives? I too long to be in a thousand places at once and do exactly as I feel— "to be exhilarated by my life instead of bearing with it."

But we can't do what we want all the time without a thought for others. Yes, I resent that sometimes. I resent my life being dictated by the endless duties of mothering. And I resent that you managed to get away—"by hook or by crook." You walked away because you weren't strong enough to handle the responsibility of family—and the messy, maddening beauty of it.

It amazes me that some of the answers have been lying all these years in this dusty folder at the back of a filing cabinet. As I read through her final letters, I see how blind I've been to her attempts to express her love and interest in me. Her letters show me now that she *was* reaching out to me, trying to see who I was and who I was becoming. She writes in a letter never sent:

> *Now, darlin'—you must write me. I want to hear about school and your friends and the animals at home. I will find it difficult to believe you aren't considering "beaus" so I want to hear about any special fellows. And please, please, let me know how you feel—I mean really feel— about my going away so suddenly and about things in general. Are you lonely or depressed, high or happy, worried, frightened, confident, pleased—all that about everything. It's "real" important.*

In her letters, I feel her presence—the beautiful, complex, and full human being she was. Her words are tangible evidence that her life mattered, that she had a voice. There are no concrete answers in her letters. There isn't really anywhere where she says "I'm sorry." But her words here are something that I can hold onto. Here is her voice—the one I yearned to hear, to understand for so many years. This is the window I can look through to glimpse her complicated, confused, bright, mindful, and longing self.

Yes, perhaps a mother is supposed to make the commitment to stick around and raise her children, and yes, that is the commitment I have made. But not my mother. She was always pulled into her own desperate soul-searching journey. And if she couldn't figure out who she was, even if she had stayed and stuck it out with my dad and with us through thick and thin, in the end how could she ever have helped us figure out who we are?

And I know from another letter never sent that she must have passed her fierce desire to write on to me.

My mother says it this way:

There is such a need, a compulsion to write. I am trying so very hard to release all that is in me—to spill my very guts so they can fall loose and be observed. What is in this body and mind of mine? This disintegration of all my self—a gurgling mass in a gutter of vomited dreams flowing silently, sinfully into oblivion. So yearning to be strong that I made a mockery of strength. So foolish, this mind of mine that must bend to the heart. Jelly, pulpy mass with no integrity. To what? If my mind cannot overcome my heart, then what good is it?

Like my mom, I write to understand myself and lure the voice inside me out of hiding. I write because of my brother Jamie, who always reached for pen and paper because he needed to draw. His voice lived inside of those drawings. Where is all his beautiful artwork now? And I write because of my grandmother Joan's journals, which sit in the drawer of my desk at home like heavy lumps of clay that longed for a shape but never got formed. I write because of my brother Eden, who once told me, "I've got a suitcase underneath my bed and it's packed, filled with story ideas, movie scripts and stuff producers are just dying to get a hold of—it's all pure gold," I don't want to die with a suitcase full of ideas underneath my bed or a hundred spiral notebooks full of stories beneath my desk. I want to set the words free, unearth what has been buried for too long. I have to believe that a leap of faith was better than standing still. I had to get the memories and stories down on paper, and if I didn't, this history would be lost or—an even worse thought—repeated. Sometimes all I have is this instinctual, obsessive need to put pen to paper—to set fire to something inside me that may or may not save me.

I pull the covers around me and settle into the slope of the mattress. It occurs to me that I've come here for the wrong reasons. I am the pitiful daughter who waited too long to reach out to my mom for answers. I got on a plane Christmas Day believing that I would come home a different person. But my mom is still alive, and I am still her longing daughter. My very presence must remind her of her failures and poor decisions. I curl into a small shape by drawing my knees to my chest. It's true: through all these years, I've yearned for that acknowledgment, but she has never been able to look at my face and say "I'm sorry," or "I'm so sorry for leaving you," or "I'm so sorry for not being there for you." Is that really all I've needed?

NOW

a few small repairs

I t's my last day here in Olympia. Outside the window, Kim is loading the truck with crates of pink and green apples to take to the farmers market.

There is so much more I need to say and fix before my mom dies. But words can only come when I have everything inside me under control. Maybe now is one of those moments when I can put on a courageous face and keep my emotions in order.

She is lying on her back, half-awake with her mouth partially open and her coarse hair damp and matted. I rest my hand on her arm, and her parched lips almost stretch into a smile. She can tell it's me.

"Mom?"

She nods.

I hold onto the edge of the blanket covering her. "Mom, I'm scared."

She keeps her eyes closed, waiting for me to continue.

I don't know what to say next. I'm waiting for her to say something to me but she doesn't, so I come up with the first thing that springs to mind, "When you're gone Mom, I'm going to plant a garden for you. With purple dahlias and mums and blue forget-me-nots."

"Oh yeah," she says. "That would be real nice."

And then there's nothing more to say. She keeps her eyes closed. I wipe mine with the back of my hand. I'm glad she doesn't open her eyes and look up at me, because having to really look at each other, eye to eye, would violate the distance we have maintained for so long. There is a loss and love so great between us that we have forbidden ourselves from truly connecting. It is simply too painful.

When Bella asked me, "What did your mom do when you were scared?" I stared up at the yellow stars on the ceiling and could not tell her the truth of who I was. How could I tell my daughter that my mom left when I was a little girl? I thought if I told Bella that, she would become afraid that I was that kind of mother too and would always be watching or waiting for me to leave. And I feared this myself. What if that leaving gene lay dormant inside me? What if something inside me snapped one day and I walked out the front door? No mother is fully immune from the possibility of leaving her children.

These thoughts are unbearable. But it is my history and I have no choice but to embrace it. I come from this circle of mothers who left their children. Grandma Rita was dropped off at a convent to be raised by Catholic nuns. Her mother couldn't take care of her. My grandmother Joan drank herself to death in her forties when her daughters still needed her. My mom's sister gave up her firstborn for adoption. By choice, my mom did not raise her three children.

My mom didn't pass a "leaving gene" on to me. I know this

now. While I feared a genetic marker could sneak up on me, I know I could not endure leaving my children. I would never be able to stitch myself back up and could never, ever forgive myself. I could never be whole again, because my children are pieces of me and I of them. Just like I am a piece of my mother, and she is a part of me—even if she couldn't recognize that.

A piece of her sorrow will always lie within me, like a shard of broken glass. There are times I feel just like her—"a dandelion blowing in a thousand directions all at once" with no idea which way to go.

I feel her when I carry my children's bodies, heavy with sleep, up the stairs. It's not always thankfulness that I feel, but resentment for the simple and relentless things she never had to do. I feel her when a glass of wine hits my bloodstream and I get that brief sensation of warmth, euphoria, and limitless possibilities. I feel her when I sit on a horse and know that she gave me my natural rider's seat and strong hands.

Kim's truck rumbles down the driveway. My time is up here. I arrived believing that I would bear witness to my mom's death, and through that, I would experience some kind of cathartic shift—an aha moment of truth. A release of all I have been holding inside me.

I know now that I'm not going to have that moment I hoped for with my mom. She's hanging on, and I'm going to keep my promise to Bella and Dominic and be back for New Year's.

I run upstairs and grab the whole file of letters never sent and stuff them into my suitcase. I will steal her letters because they are the most intimate pieces I will ever have of her.

My flight leaves this afternoon. I will travel through the turbulent sky 960 miles to my family where I belong.

NOW

leaving olympia

Thirty-six years have passed since I watched my mom drive away in her baby-blue Dodge Dart. I've played that memory over in my head a thousand times, wondering: if I only had called out to her, was there any way she might have stayed? In the end she always drives away and I am left standing at the windowsill—waiting.

This time, my mom has gathered the last of her strength and come to the window. She is standing on the other side looking out at me, her hand against the glass, open like a pale starfish. I am sitting in a red rental car outside her house in the rain, staring straight at her. She is searching for my face through the heavy downpour.

I know this is the last image I will have of her. Ever. I will not see her again in this lifetime.

She balances herself against the edge of a table cluttered with a collection of treasures—ceramic frogs, seashells, and clay figures from Mexico. Her hand presses against the window glass and I lift mine against the window of the car. The outside world wobbles in the rain, and it seems like we can almost reach each other.

I hold on to every bit of her—her blue eyes; the wavy hair

surrounding her angular face; the texture of her sweater, dark and bumpy like the skin of a ripe avocado. Rivulets of rain run down the window in front of her, making her appear like an Impressionist painting. A Pissarro or Cézanne in later years. The palette is yellow, cerulean blue, and deep umber. She is still alive, standing to wave good-bye to me. But her body is shutting down, a firefly flickering in the distant woods.

I wrap my fingers around the door handle. I'm so close. I could reach her in six or seven seconds. But I can't run back in one more time. I have a plane to catch. A rental car that's on empty and needs returning. My family is counting on me coming home tonight. We will ring in the new year with our tradition of banging kitchen pots and pans and lighting sparklers in the backyard.

I turn the key. My mom is still at the window, her hand still against the glass. Underwater, everything is quiet and full of ripples. There is so much more than sawdust inside Bun-Bun and me. There always was.

I am the one driving away this time.

Her letters offer me comfort now.

My darlin', my Lou,

May it never be too painful for you to look inside and to share all that you find within. There is so much beauty in you that it would be selfish to lock it away. And beauty includes any pain or anger—all things must have balance.

I wouldn't trade my mom for any other in the world.

My hands clutch the top of the steering wheel too tightly, and blue-green veins spread out like a map under my pale skin. I look in the rearview mirror. My mom is still waiting at the window.

As my hand touches the turn signal to bear right, I feel my mouth break open like a fish gasping for air, opening and closing. I push my foot against the pedal and feel the car surge forward. There is the strong scent of evergreen and wet earth all around me. Olympia is a beautiful place to die.

epilogue

I was between errands, after dropping the kids off at school, when the call came that my mom had died in the night. Though I already knew it was coming, there was nothing to ease the impact. I felt raw and skinned. Exhausted from waiting.

I tried to imagine her departure. Strangers pushing her out of the house. White sheets surrounding her like a cocoon. Could she grow wings and transform herself into a butterfly or a blue-winged teal?

I imagined the gurney clunking over the floorboards as they wheeled her out of the bedroom and past the carving of the flying owl in the living room. Or maybe they took her out by way of the back patio and past the dying apple tree instead. I will never know because these are not the questions I will ever ask Kim. He was the one who belonged with her on the day she died.

Kim asked me if I could call my dad and brothers. But I couldn't do it right away. I felt an intense need to run—fast and uphill. Before calling anyone with the news, I drove to the base of a steep grade in Los Angeles and sprinted up the wide path like a seasoned runner. I sprinted as if I could outrun the truth. As my feet scrambled over gravel and dirt, I believed that I could still reach my mom. She might still be somewhere in the transition between the dark soil and the flat, gray sky. After all, she had always been like that, a wandering soul.

When I reached the top of the hill, my throat burned like I had swallowed a fistful of salt. I focused on the gray sky overhead.

"Can you hear me, Mom? I'm here. Goddamn it, I'm here. Please give me a sign, *anything.*"

I stood on the top of that wet green hill waiting for something in the universe to shift. A breeze, a subtle change of light, a snap of a branch, a rustle in the grass. But nothing moved. The sky held its gray, cold and hard like river rock.

I sat on the ground and pounded my fists against the dirt. I pleaded one last time, "Can you just tell me that everything is going to be *okay?*"

Silence and stillness. She was gone.

As soon as I got back to the bottom of the hill, I called my dad and brothers. When I reached Eden with the news, his voice was gentle and resigned. Then he relayed a story I had never heard before about his last visit with Mom.

"Mom and me, we did our fifth step together before she died. We made a list of all our wrongdoings so we could make amends to all the people we have hurt. I sat at the foot of her bed and made a list, and she made hers. It was the AA step that both of us had been avoiding for a long time. Even though she had kind of given up on AA and could never really give up the drinking, she knew that she had to do this step."

Eden said they confessed all their regrets and wrongdoings in one sitting. They wrote them out on paper and then burned them in a stainless-steel cooking pot out on the deck. I tried to imagine the two of them watching the fire that could burn up all their mistakes so quickly.

I was glad that my brother felt this sense of closure with her, but I had to say what I thought.

"That's great that you got to have that experience with Mom, but I have to tell you that she didn't make amends with me. She never really said she was sorry for things that truly hurt."

"That's not true," he said. Then he turned his words carefully, tuning them like he was reading them from a sacred text or giving an intimate lecture.

"You don't know how people make their amends. You may think you do. You may believe that it's by saying words like 'sorry' or 'I wish I could have been a different person.' But sometimes amends comes in other ways—ways you *never* expect. Think about it. Her amends might somehow be tied to the fact that you have a great family and two healthy kids. There are no rules when it comes to forgiveness. Her amends might be in something that you don't even know about yet—something *huge* that's coming."

I looked back at the hillside I had climbed up. There was no sign of her whatsoever. All I had were my brother's words. I took them and tucked them away. Because what did any of us really know anyway. Who's to say how these things work in the world?

In the weeks after she died I found myself unable to identify a single emotion. Unmoored, I drifted through the days, unaware of what was shifting inside me. Grief was charting its own course.

Within the space of fourteen days, cells began dividing

rapidly inside me. And dividing again. And then news that seemed impossible—*huge*. A tiny heart, smaller than a flower seed, was beginning to form. I was pregnant.

I cried. I wailed like I never had before. *This cannot be happening*, I thought. *I cannot have a baby. Aren't I finally supposed to have the time to pursue the dreams I put on hold throughout the years of parenting my first two children?*

My mind retreated to the conversation I had with the stranger on the plane on Christmas Day, who had asked me if I was going to have any more kids. "God, no. My kids are big now, nine and twelve," I'd told him smugly. This I was certain of. There was no way I was going to start all over again. There was no way I was going to be the mother of three children.

But when I saw the black and white heart beating in the ultrasound image, I felt my mom skipping around inside me. I felt her blue eyes open wide. There were no more questions. No sign could have knocked me off my feet harder.

I often go back to that morning on the hilltop—when the sky seemed unyielding and I asked for something, anything to shift in the universe. And I see now that some kind of magic occurred between the earth and the sky that day. Maybe I chose it. Maybe she chose it. Maybe neither of us did. All I know for sure is that eight months and seventeen days after my mom died, I was holding a baby in my arms. This was the unexpected miracle, the sign that swept me off my feet.

Do I see my mom when I look at my young son's bright blue eyes and unfurl his tiny fingers? Yes, sometimes I do.

reading group guide

1. The action of *Pieces of My Mother* alternates between Melissa's final days with her mother in 2007, and the story of Melissa's childhood, which ranges over a number of years. Did you find one storyline more intriguing than the other? Were you eager to get back to one or the other?

2. In what ways does Melissa use her imagination as a child to escape her pain and longing for her mother?

3. Do you know any mothers who have left a child or a family behind to pursue a different life? What about father who has left their family?

4. As a child, Melissa chooses friends who have separated or divorced parents. Unlike Melissa, most of her friends live with their mothers, rather than with their fathers. Do you think our society is more accepting of fathers who leave their families behind? How does our society view mothers who abandon children by choice?

5. As she is growing up, Melissa collects various knickknacks and treasures. She displays them in her room, carefully cleaning and rearranging them. Later she says, "I give value and meaning to ephemera and small objects." Why does Melissa focus so much on the treasures in her room? How are the objects more reliable than the people in her life?

6. Melissa describes her and her brothers as a tribe of three. With an absent mother, working father, and live-in sitters that come and go, Melissa and her brothers learn to rely on each other in childhood. How does this bond carry through adulthood? Are there points when the siblings' bond wavers?

7. What are the unique traits Melissa develops by growing up in a house of boys with frequent live-ins?

8. How do the addictions and alcoholism that surround Melissa as a child impact her?

9. As a teen, Melissa yearns to connect with brothers by adapting some of their behaviors—like being more daring and troublesome. Does she succeed in getting the attention she is seeking?

10. At what point does the girl Melissa lose hope that her mother will return to the family, resuming a traditional mother role?

11. What traits does Melissa seem to inherit from her mother? From her father?

12. Why do you think Melissa's mother chose to keep a file hidden and marked "letters never sent," rather than sending them? How do the letters that Melissa's mother "never sent" help inform the story?

13. What similarities do you find in Melissa's prose and her mother's letters?

14. During her mother's final days, Melissa says, "There is so much more I need to say and fix before my mom dies. But words can only come when I have everything inside me under control." The last words she says to her mother are about planting a garden in her memory. Do you feel that Melissa ultimately finds closure with her mother in their last exchange?

15. In adulthood, Melissa frequently questions her abilities as a mother. "I am trying so hard to the right things, to be a good mother," she relates. And, "When I interact with other mothers on the school yard, I feel transparent." Do you think Melissa would be more confident today if she had grown up with her mother, rather than apart from her?

16. If you could write a letter to anyone in your family or from your past—who would it be and what would you say to them? Would you send it?

a conversation with
the author

Can you tell us a bit more of the backstory behind this book? What did you hope to achieve by exploring this particular topic in a memoir?

The story really started when I became a mother. I was head-over-heels in love with this new baby of mine and I wondered, *How could a mother leave her child?* I needed to make sense of how my mother—how any mother—could abandon her children. I had to look at where I had come from, which was a long line of complicated women. I wanted to do what no other woman in my family was able to do—tell her own story. I wanted to give a voice to these generations of women who had so far remained voiceless.

Did you experiment with different structures or ways of telling your story? What made you decide to narrate it through alternating chapters of past and present?

Yes, I tried many different ways to tell my story. At first, I didn't want to write it as a memoir. In fact, I originally wrote it as fiction, but I struggled with that because ultimately I couldn't get away from the truth. My memories of early childhood are nearly photographic and those vivid recollections remained with me during the writing process. As far as narrating through alternating chapters, that structure came later, after my mom died. I realized I was trying to tell two stories: one of my childhood and one of my mother's final days. When I put this structure in place, it made sense. It allowed me to tell both the past and the present.

You write openly and candidly about a subject that is very painful for most people to discuss. What were some of the challenges and benefits of this?

I don't feel I had a choice about whether to write this book— it was a story that just keep pulling me to create it. It's something that's very painful, yes, but it felt necessary. It's certainly a challenge to go into those places. It can be emotionally depleting. And the deeper you dig, the tougher it gets emotionally. One of the greatest challenges was to find the balance between motherhood and writing about my own mother. I often felt starved for time to write and also guilty about the time it would take away from my children. I worried I was being selfish. I hope that one day my children will see my perseverance as a strong trait. The editing process was also a challenge; it was hard for me to go back into this narrative again and again. I worked on this story for twelve years. My children were young and my mother was dying as I wrote.

What is the biggest lesson you learned from publishing the book?

Perseverance. I had so many opportunities to give up on this story. And over the course of twelve years, I wrote a lot of what Anne Lamott calls sh***y first drafts. I had many rejections along the way, but I never really gave up. I had to keep shifting my perspective and trust there was reason I was so determined. The second lesson came after I finally found a publisher—and this had to do with letting go of the story. This was hard for me because I realized that I could keep tinkering with the book for another ten years. It was never going to be "good enough" or nearly perfect, and I needed to accept that and let it go out into the world no matter the outcome or criticism.

What would you like readers to gain from reading *Pieces of My Mother*? Any advice or life lessons they should take away in particular?

It is in telling our truths that we find forgiveness. I think it's important to tell our stories, as hard or challenging as that might be. And the process of doing so can help us to heal and also find compassion. One lesson I would love readers to take away is that it's so important to say the things you want to say to your loved ones during this lifetime and show them they are valued. It would be wonderful if some readers felt compelled to reach out and write a letter to someone they've loved. Why should we leave this world with "letters never sent"?

What advice would you give to someone who is struggling to repair a relationship with one or both of their parents?

We're all flawed and broken in our own ways, and it's important to acknowledge our own shortcomings and our own roles in difficult situations. When we take away that judgment, we can see the other person more fully, more wholly, and begin to repair our bond with them. Try to find a way to forgive, no matter what it takes. It's not easy but it's the right thing to do, and it's how we grow. Life is too brief to hold on to past hurts.

You work at the renowned independent bookstore Book Passage, so you're clearly passionate about books. Did you know you wanted to write a book as well?

I am incredibly passionate about books; working at Book Passage is a dream job. It puts me in a like-minded community and constantly nourishes and inspires me. It couldn't be a better match for an aspiring writer. When I started working at Book Passage, I had a draft of my book done. But I decided to put that draft in a drawer for a year and become immersed in the world of books and authors. I kept a file on my desktop called "Gifts from Book Passage." I often took notes at author events that resonated with me. It seemed that every event I hosted was a reminder to me that I could be a writer—if I didn't give up.

What are your favorite genres to read? What did you read while you were writing this book?

I read a lot of literary fiction, short stories, memoirs, essays, and poetry. I particularly love short stories (so much that I asked George Saunders to sign my arm in black Sharpie). I appreciate writers who use unique and stunning language or are just great storytellers. That said, I tried not to read too many memoirs while I was working on this book.

How would you describe your writing style in a couple words?

Spare, emotional, and introspective.

Which person in the book do you feel most closely connected to?

This is tough to answer because it makes me name only one member of my family. The person who I had to examine the most fully, of course, was my mother, so through reading her journals and her letters I came to know a part of her that I didn't know outside of those words. She was the hardest to understand, of course. I hope that this book might also be a love letter to my mother, a way to honor her remarkable spirit.

acknowledgments

I began writing this story when my daughter was four. She's almost seventeen now. That leaves me with a tremendous number of people to thank and not nearly enough pages to adequately express my immense gratitude.

I am deeply grateful to those who read early first drafts of this story and provided me with invaluable insight—Jackie Casey, Martina Cistaro, Adrienne Coppola, Mark Donnelly, Hope Edelman, Amy Friedman, Susan Hillenbrand, Abigail Jones, Liz Kiely, Deborah Lott, Kathy Lorentz, Helen Storey, Christine Schwab, Alison Randall, and Sam Roberson.

Endless gratitude for the incredible people in my life who have continued to inspire me throughout this journey: Joan Chapin, Monica Golden, Asiya Hassan, Lisa Marvier, Kirsten McCormick, Darlene Mininni, JP Reynolds, Johanna Rupp, and Jeri Stoeber.

Monica Holloway and Liz Berman, what would I do without your friendship and encouragement over the years? Thank you Heather Young for saying yes and helping me with edits in those final frantic hours. Thank you Kate Milliken and Adam Karsten.

I was truly lucky to stumble upon the guidance of Arielle

Eckstut and David Henry Sterry—two of the nicest and most generous people in the publishing world.

I am indebted to the many writers and teachers who encouraged me along the way, including the wise and wonderful Barbara Abercrombie, Samantha Chang, Leslie Keenan, Anne Lamott, and Corey Mandell. Steve Wolfson, you cannot imagine how profoundly your encouragement years ago helped me to keep writing.

Laurie Fox, thank you for putting your faith in this story and guiding me through every step. You are a kindred spirit and agent extraordinaire.

Stephanie Bowen, thank you for your keen eyes and big heart in helping me answer the most difficult questions during the editing process. And special thanks to the talented team at Sourcebooks for welcoming me with such enthusiasm and dedication—especially Liz Kelsch, Lathea Williams, Chris Bauerle, Rachel Kahn, Adrienne Krogh, Heather Moore, Sean Murray, Valerie Pierce, Dominique Raccah, Helen Scott, and Heidi Weiland.

This story would not exist without the support of my family. I am blessed with the best true-blue hippie dad a daughter could ever ask for. Jamie and Eden, I marvel at your kindness, humor and compassion. I am ever-grateful to my beautiful mother, who recently ambled over to me in a dream, whole again, and hugged me with great tenderness. This is how I'd like to remember her. Thank you Kim Baxter for taking such good care of Mom over the years.

Many thanks to the amazing staff and events team at Book Passage. Thank you Karen West for your spirited and generous insights, Calvin Crosby for ushering me in, and Elaine and Bill Petrocelli for owning the greatest book store in the world—a place that feels like home to me in so many ways.

I'd also like to thank the talented writers who generously offered to read galleys prior to publication: Tom Barbash, Kelly Corrigan, Katie Hafner, Caroline Leavitt, Cheryl McKeon, Peter Orner, Will Schwalbe, Abigail Thomas, Ayelet Waldman, and Lolly Winston. And as far-reaching as it may seem, I want to thank every author I've had the privilege of meeting and introducing at Book Passage. Each experience remains a gift—a rare glimpse into the creative process and the wonderful, complex journey of writing and publishing books. I remain in awe of every writer who dares to write down the stories in their hearts and imaginations.

Lastly, for my children—Dominic, Bella, and Gianmarco—you are the sun, the moon, and the stars. And Anthony, your unwavering support for my work astonishes me and reminds me how lucky in love I am.

about the author

Melissa Cistaro is a bookseller and events coordinator at Book Passage, the legendary San Francisco Bay Area independent bookstore, where she has hosted more than two hundred authors. A writer and mother, her work has been published in numerous literary journals including the *New Ohio Review*, *Anderbo.com*, and *Brevity*, as well as in the anthologies *Love and Profanity* and *Cherished*, alongside Anne Lamott and Jane Smiley and other writers. Melissa graduated with honors from UCLA and continued her education with the UCLA Extension Writers' Program and at the Tin House Writer's Workshop in Portland.